The Way of the Cross

by

Larry D. Rudder

TO JOE:

Larry D. Rudder

RudderHaven

3014 Washington Ave

Granite City, IL 62040

Published by:
RudderHaven
3014 Washington Ave
Granite City, IL 62040
USA

First Softcover Printing, May 2015, RudderHaven
(978-1-932060-15-7)

Copyright © 2015 Larry D. Rudder

All Rights Reserved

Cover Design: Sheri L. Rudder

*Neither the artist, the author, nor the publisher make any claim to any and
all third-party 3D models, textures, or other materials used in the creation
of the cover art. All copyrights for third-party materials belong to the individual creators and/or producers of those materials. Used under license. The
artist only claims the copyright of the finished derivative art.*

Printed in the United States of America

ISBN 978-1-932060-15-7

No part of this publication may be reproduced, stored in or introduced into
a retrieval system, or transmitted, in any form, or by any means (electronic,
mechanical, photocopying, recording, or otherwise), without the prior written permission of both the copyright owner and the above publisher of this
book.

A Special Thanks. . . .

To the editors and publishers in my family who spent many hours preparing the manuscript for publication.

To my wife, Jeanette (M.A.), who spent more time on my work than on her own in editing and proofing the complete manuscript.

To my sons, Douglas and Jonathan, who prepared the manuscript for publication, including editing, layout, and design.

To my daughter-in-law, Sheri, who designed the cover art.

Contents

1. The Way of the Cross Begins

A Winding Path Made Straight................................1
The Cost of Discipleship...11
Prepared for the Battle..16
An Army of Sheep...26
The Way of Truth...31
The Way of Life..40

2. He Called Him "My Master"

Meet for the Master's Use...49
He is Lord!..57
Are You Acceptable?..63
A New and Living Way...73
Examine Yourself...90

3. From Darkness to Light

Out of Darkness...103
A Candle in the Night..111
A Myriad of Candles...116
The Children of Light..120
A New Way of Thinking..133
The Promise of the Father..139
A New and Living Way...147

4. It All Began With Love

The Joy in Knowing Jesus......................................165
Joy Fulfilled...177
The Groundswell of Joy.....................................180
The Law of Christ..190

5. The Way of the Cross Made Plain

The Way of the Cross Made Plain...........................195

The Way of the Cross Begins

If any man will come after me, let him deny himself, and take up his cross, and follow me.

—Matthew 16:24—

A Winding Path Made Straight:

I am the voice of one crying in the wilderness, Make straight the way of the Lord. [John 1:23]

My favorite portion of Scripture is found in the fourteenth chapter of John's Gospel. I quote it often in my preaching ministry. Jesus said, "Let not your heart be troubled: ye believe in God, believe also in me. In my Father's house are many mansions: if it were not so, I would have told you. I go to prepare a place for you. And if I go and prepare a place for you, I will come again, and receive you unto myself; that where I am, there ye may be also. And whither I go ye know, and the way ye know. Thomas saith unto him, Lord, we know not whither thou goest; and how can we know the way? Jesus saith unto him, *I am the way, the truth*, and *the life*: no man cometh unto the Father, but by me" (John 14:1–6). Those three attributes of Christ above are essential to our journey through this life if we expect to enter the gates of Glory.

Every Billy Graham Crusade displayed the first sentence of John 14:6, in which Jesus told His disciples, "I am the way, the truth, and the life." What was not included in the sign was the rest of the verse: "No man cometh unto the Father but by me." That always seemed strange to me. I thought that an evangelist would want to use the evangelistic part of the verse.

When I was a young *Youth for Christ* director I had the same verse displayed on the stage at the local junior high school at every Saturday-night rally, but I had two signs painted. On one side of the stage the sign gave the

1

first sentence, and on the other side of the stage, it gave the closing sentence. I felt then, as I do now, that the whole verse must remain intact!

The three terms, the way, the truth, and the life, are applied to the Lord Jesus Christ in the first chapter of John's Gospel. Christ as the Truth is found in verse 17: "For the law was given by Moses, but grace and *truth* came by Jesus Christ." We find Christ presented as *the Life* in verse 4: "In him was life; and *the life* was the light of men."

Citing Isaiah 40:3, John the Baptist said of himself, "I am the voice of one crying in the wilderness." His cry pointed to Jesus as the Way: "Make straight *the way* of the Lord [referring to Jesus]" (John 1:23). In verse 36, John pointed two of his disciples to the Way saying, "Behold the Lamb of God!" The way of the Lord is the way to life everlasting, and the way to everlasting life is *the way of the cross.*

It is no wonder that believers were not first called Christians but rather "followers of the Way." As Acts 11:26 tells us, "And the disciples were called Christians first in Antioch" nine years after Pentecost.

The figure of Christ in Genesis is found in Genesis 3:24. After Adam and Eve disobeyed the Lord, bringing death upon themselves and all the other creatures, the Lord cast them out of the Garden of Eden, as we are told in the verse: "So he drove out the man; and he placed at the east of the garden of Eden Cherubims, and a flaming sword which turned every way, to keep the way of the tree of life."

As I share the following information with you, I want you to keep in mind that there was a number of real cherubim in Genesis 3 that the Lord placed at the entrance to the garden. There was also a real sword that was ablaze with fire that turned in every direction "to keep the way of the tree of life." Contrary to what most people believe, the Bible does not say that an angel was holding the sword and swinging it in circles! However, the term *flaming sword* has a double meaning in the Hebrew language. It is used to describe the actual weapon we call a sword that is ablaze with fire, but the Hebrew word used for the first term "flaming" also means "to be enwrapped as if by magic." At first glance one might see that as fairytale language, but it was the only way to describe to common folk that a sword wrapped in a glorious blaze of fire was standing alone and turning in every direction without the aid of anyone. The Hebrew word for "sword" also means "to be parched (as by drought)." As a *type* or picture, one could easily understand this to mean that Adam and Eve were cut off from Eden by a contingent of cherubim positioned at the east end of the garden, the only entryway, and committed to a land of drought—a spiritual drought that results in death. Why? To keep the way of the tree of life—the way of the cross of Christ! Remember, I speak regarding types or illustrations of a greater meaning, and do not deny for one second that there was a real flaming sword that blocked the entryway to Eden.

Had the sinful couple partaken of the tree of life, they would have lived forever in sin. But there is no life in sin; sin can only bring death. I suppose one could say that they would have been what Hollywood calls "the living dead," and that, indeed, is true of the entire human race apart from the saving grace of God through the sacrifice of His Son. There would never have been peace, joy, and love for all eternity. There would have been no relationship at all with the Lord, who had been with them each day in the garden. It was, however, God's plan to redeem them through the gift of His Son on the cross—the true tree of Life!

So let's look first at Christ's reference to Himself as *the way*. When Jesus said that He is the way, He made it clear that He is the *only* way to eternal life and the kingdom of God. He said, "No man cometh unto the Father but by me." No other religion will get us to Heaven. All others belong to this world and the prince of this world. He warns us in Matthew 7:13–14, "Enter ye in at the strait gate: for wide is the gate, and broad is the way, that leadeth to destruction, and many there be which go in thereat: Because strait is the gate, and narrow is the way, which leadeth unto life, and *few* there be that find it."

The way of the cross is a narrow path that follows the footsteps of the Master, but the church of today, the church of the end times, doesn't recognize that because it has become apostate. It has turned from the way of the cross to follow the way of the world. Those are the only two paths laid out before us. Sadly, the majority of people have chosen the wrong path. Solomon warned us that "there is a way which seemeth right unto a man, but the end thereof are the ways of death" (Proverbs 14:12). Where the religious man is concerned, he added in verse 14, "The backslider in heart shall be filled with *his own ways*." The way of the cross is not an easy way because it is the way that Christ has laid out for us to follow. It is *His* way, *not ours*.

4

Jesus tells us exactly what is meant by the "strait gate" in John 10:9: "I am the door [gate]: by me if any man enter in, he shall be saved, and shall go in and out, and find pasture." Christ is also the "narrow way" which "leadeth unto life." While most people choose to believe that they can make it through this life and into the next their own way, their own religion, their own good deeds, or their own money, they are without any hope at all.

There is that "flaming sword" that stands between them and entrance through that narrow gate. Hebrews 1:6–8 tells us of a contingent of angels who protect the narrow gate and the One who opens the door. "And again, when he [God] bringeth in [literally: *bringeth back*] the first begotten into the world, he saith, And let all the angels of God worship him. And of the angels he saith, Who maketh his angels spirits, and his ministers a flame of fire. But unto the Son, Thy throne, O God, is forever and ever: a sceptre of righteousness is the sceptre of thy kingdom."

Of these angels, verse 14 tells us, "Are they not all ministering spirits sent forth to minister for them who shall be heirs of salvation?" In the case of the way of the cross, the way of salvation, God has sent His angels to guide our paths to the entryway of the Paradise of God (as implied by Luke 16:22 where we are told that angels carried Lazarus to the bosom of Abraham upon the beggar's death), where Jesus stands with sceptre in hand to authorize our entrance. He is, after all, the door of the sheepfold. He said, "I am the door: by me if any man enter in, he shall be saved, and shall go in and out, and find pasture" (John 10:9).

Concerning those errant souls who attempt to enter another way, Jesus said, "Verily, verily, I say unto you, He that entereth not by the door into the sheepfold, but climbeth up some other way, the same is a thief and a robber" (John 10:1), and the thief and the robber cannot come to the Father because they can only come through the door of the sheepfold.

Years ago, I lived near a starch factory that had a high chain link fence around it. Railroad tracks went into the factory grounds where boxcars were loaded with barrels and sacks of cornstarch. A young teenager decided to climb the fence one night when the factory was idle. No one knows why he chose to sneak into the facility, but he broke a lock on a boxcar door, entered the car and found several railroad flares. He stole the flares, took them home, and attempted to use them to make a model rocket. What he actually wound up making was a pipe bomb. In the process, the bomb went off, and the boy lost his legs.

Like that boy, the one who attempts to enter Heaven any way but the way of the cross will be judged as a thief and a robber. Such a person will not just lose his or her legs, but his or her soul.

When we realize that the vast majority of people on this earth will never confess Christ as their Lord, we can more readily understand what Jesus meant when He said that few would find life because they refuse to trust and follow the narrow way. It's a dangerous decision to make when one tries to climb over the fence to reach Heaven. There are those who call Christians many negative names for our narrow view that Christ is the only way to Heaven, but our Lord set the rules and made it plain.

Muslims, Buddhists, cultists, atheists, even Jews without Christ, and those of all other religions of the world will spend eternity in the lake of fire because they reject Christ as the only way to eternal life. That includes multiplied millions of lost souls.

Our Lord has shown time and again just what it takes to inherit eternal life. One of the best illustrations in the Bible is found in Mark 10:17–21 in which Christ was confronted by a wealthy young ruler of the Jews. As the Lord walked along the road, the man "came running, and kneeled to him, and asked him, Good Master, what shall I do that I may inherit eternal life?" (10:17).

This man may have been among the Pharisees who had tested Jesus concerning divorce under the law of Moses in verses 2–12. He may also have witnessed how Jesus took the little children that had been brought to Him, blessing them, and challenging the people with the simple message: "Whosoever shall not receive the kingdom of God as a little child, he shall not enter therein" (10:15).

It was as He departed that scene that the rich man ran to catch up with the Lord Jesus, fell on his knees, and asked the question that seemed so simple and yet became so complicated. I think his concerns were based on what Jesus said about the children. After all, this man was very wealthy and perhaps an intellectual of his day. He was clever enough at an early age to attain a position of great importance to the Jews. In his heart, he may have wondered how a naive little child could have more value than a rich and powerful man like himself.

He was no different from those today who place all of their confidence in their wealth and mock those who place their trust in Christ. I am reminded of the time my wife and I were invited to a Thanksgiving dinner, and the host's wife asked me to "return thanks." I offered a brief prayer of thanksgiving for the bounteous meal our Lord had placed before us. No sooner had I said, "amen," than the host glared at me and asked, "Why did you thank the Lord for the meal? I'm the one who paid for the food!"

I tried to be gracious when I responded with words to this effect, "If it weren't for our Creator there would be no food for you to purchase. After all, He created the fowl of the air, the herb yielding seed, the fruit tree yielding fruit, and everything else that went into this meal. He gave you the ability to earn the money you used to buy the stuff and the taste buds that enable you to enjoy it all." The man blew a snort through his nose and offered a sarcastic grimace.

The rich man who had chased after Jesus had the same problem. Nonetheless, he recognized that Jesus was someone with obvious authority and miraculous power. He ran to catch up with Him and fell on his knees—an expression of obeisance. He saw Jesus as a greater man than even he could be.

Likewise, our Lord's response was a heartfelt one. The Scripture states that He loved him, and He was ready and willing to answer the man, but Jesus also knew the man's heart. With God, there are no hidden secrets. He knew exactly what the young man was thinking, and His first response was to ask, "Why callest thou me good? There is none good but one, that is, God" (10:18). If the young man truly believed that Jesus was "good," then he must also believe that Jesus was God for only God could tell him how to inherit eternal life. Then Jesus tested him further, reminding him of the ten commandments that God had given to Moses, to which the young man said, "Master, all these have I observed from my youth" (10:20).

"Then Jesus beholding him loved him, and said unto him, one thing thou lackest: go thy way, sell whatsoever thou hast, and give to the poor, and thou shalt have treasure in heaven: and come, take up the cross, and follow me" (10:21).

The rich young ruler was anxious to gain an eternal inheritance, but he was not willing to follow the One who owns the treasury of Heaven because he could not trade his worldly wealth for the cross of Christ. In other words, he could not yield to the Lordship of Jesus Christ.

I mentioned earlier that the way of the cross is not an easy way because it is the way of Christ. You see, the Roman authorities required those who spoke against Caesar to carry a heavy cross through the city as a punishment for their disrespect for the god of Rome (being Caesar). The young man was not aware of the horror of the cross that Jesus would soon experience, but he knew what it meant to carry the cross, and I'm sure that was on his mind. He also knew what it meant to give up his great wealth, so when Jesus told him how to achieve the goal he was seeking, he hung his head and walked away. "He was sad at that saying, and went away grieved: for he had great possessions" (10:22). His earthly wealth was more important to him than any eternal reward, and he was certainly not willing to follow the way of the cross—the ultimate tree of life.

The ironic thing about the rich man's approach is that he was very wealthy and powerful and still saw Jesus as a man who was far superior to him. Yet any normal person would only have seen that Jesus was a man with no obvious possessions and no earthly authority. Jesus said, "Foxes have holes, and the birds of the air have nests; but the Son of man hath not where to lay his head" (Luke 9:58). He even commanded His disciples in Mark 6:8–9 that "they should take nothing for their journey, save a staff only; no scrip [a leather pouch for food], no bread, no money in their purse: But be shod with sandals; and not put on two coats" as they went out to witness to the lost. He told them in Luke 9:23, "If any man will come after me, let him *deny himself*, and *take up his cross daily*, and *follow me*."

The Cost of Discipleship:

*If any man come to me, and hate not his father,
and mother, and wife, and children, and brethren,
and sisters, yea, and his own life also, he cannot
be my disciple.* **[Luke 14:26]**

As exemplified by the rich young ruler, there are three
characteristics of a true disciple of Jesus Christ—self-
denial, carrying the message of the cross publicly every
day of our lives, and following Jesus by yielding our lives
to His leadership and ownership, making Him the Lord
of our lives. When we fail in any of these three areas, we
fall short of what God requires of us. Let's think about
that first condition: Deny yourself. Paul said of himself,
"But what things were gain to me, those I counted loss
for Christ. Yea doubtless, and I count all things but loss
for the excellency of the knowledge of Christ Jesus my
Lord: for whom I have suffered the loss of all things,
and do count them but dung, that I may win Christ"
(Philippians 3:7–8). If your worldly possessions come
between you and your commitment to Christ, you have
missed "the mark for the prize of the high calling of God
in Christ Jesus" (Philippians 3:14). Paul compares the
loss of his worldly possessions for the sake of Christ and
the message of the cross with spreading the droppings of
cattle in the fields—no more value than that!

If you fail to take up your cross daily, you deny the
gospel to the lost and your testimony before your fellow
believers. Jesus said that "whosoever doth not bear his
cross, and come after me, cannot be my disciple" (Luke
14:27). Are you a disciple of Christ? According to our

Lord Jesus, you cannot be His disciple unless you bear your cross and follow Him. He went on to say in verse 33, "So likewise, whosoever he be of you that forsaketh not all that he hath he cannot be my disciple." Our Lord expects us to place Him above all else in our lives, and anything that stands between you and your service to Him is unacceptable. He must be the most important and time-consuming person in your life. Do you have a problem with that? If you do, it is time to re-evaluate your relationship with Christ!

Following the way of the cross requires us to carry the burden of the cross both to those who are without the hope of salvation and those we hold to be true believers. Why do you think Christ's demand that he carry the cross daily was so repugnant to the rich young ruler? The man knew that if he were to share the gospel of Christ with his peers, it could cost him his life. But that is precisely what Jesus Christ requires of all those who claim His name! We are expected to give our lives to and for Him!

That does not mean by giving your life to and for Him that you will be expected to suffer and die on His account, but for some it does. If you think that is asking too much of any believer, then you must negate the heroic acts of men and women who suffer or die for their country, or those who perished in their efforts to rescue the thousands who died in the fiery attack on the twin towers of the Trade Center, or those who sacrificed themselves to establish this nation, or those who died for freedom during the Civil War, or the man on the street who ran into a burning building to save a child, or the missionaries who gave their lives to win the lost to Christ in Ecuador, Africa, and other foreign lands.

The list can go on and on, and if you think that is too much to ask, then you must be willing to accept a world where humanity would be in slavery to every dictator that comes along, and you would be willing to deny salvation to many thousands who were lost before they were ever given a chance to hear the Gospel of Christ! You see, when we truly place our faith in Christ, we die to sin that we may live in Him, and the world cannot accept such a commitment to Christ.

This brings us to that third demand that we follow Christ. Failure to follow Him constitutes a denial of His Lordship. Hebrews 12:1–2 admonishes us that we are to "lay aside every weight, and the sin which doth so easily beset us, and let us run with patience the race that is set before us, Looking unto Jesus the author and finisher of our faith; who for the joy that was set before him endured the cross, despising the shame, and is set down at the right hand of God." Notice that He considered it a joy to suffer the agony and shame of the cross knowing that it would result in giving eternal life to multiplied millions who would place their trust in Him. Jesus said that "there is joy in the presence of the angels of God over one sinner that repenteth" (Luke 15:10).

When we fail in any of the three requirements for discipleship given in Luke 9:23, we are in dire need of a spiritual checkup, a self-evaluation regarding our relationship with Christ through prayer, or what the Bible calls *seeking His face* as David said in 1 Chronicles 16:11, "Seek the Lord in his strength, seek his face continually," and immersing ourselves in the Word of God. When we fail to maintain that relationship, we stray from the way of the cross and become entangled in the briar patches of this world. One of those Old Testament types is given in Numbers 21. It is a clear type of the way of the cross. Moses was instructed by God to lead the Hebrew children out of Egypt, freeing them from the terrible bondage, the harsh slavery, they had experienced during the reign of terror that Egypt's Pharaoh had placed them under. They were promised a land flowing with milk and honey at the end of their journey through the wilderness, but Numbers 21 tells us that they were not willing to follow the way God had prepared for them. They were impatient—not willing to accept the easier burden that God had placed in their path.

The Lord had provided them with manna, the perfect bread from Heaven, to sustain them on their journey to the Promised Land. Exodus 16:2–5 gives the account: "And the whole congregation of the children of Israel murmured against Moses and Aaron in the wilderness: And the children of Israel said unto them, Would to God we had died by the hand of the Lord in the land of Egypt, when we sat by the flesh pots, and when we did eat bread to the full; for ye have brought us forth into this wilderness, to kill this whole assembly with hunger. Then said the Lord unto Moses, Behold, I will rain bread from heaven for you; and the people shall go out and gather a certain rate every day, that I may prove them, whether they will walk in my law, or no. And it shall come to pass, that on the sixth day they shall prepare that which they bring in; and it shall be twice as much as they gather daily."

What a marvelous gift that God in His mercy and love had given to Israel during their years of wandering, a time in the wilderness that was unnecessary had they been obedient children! They were a rebellious bunch, but when they cried for God's mercy, He gave them bread from Heaven. But notice that the Lord had made a certain stipulation for them if they were to continue in His blessings. They would have to yield to His Lordship. He would give them a litmus test—"prove them, whether they will walk in my law, or no." The simple fact is that had they been obedient to the Lord, He would have gladly poured out continual blessings upon them.

During their time in the wilderness, they never went hungry, their clothing never wore out. Their every need was met, but they were not willing to commit themselves to following the way as it was laid out for them by God under the leadership of Moses. Like most people today—even among those who call themselves Christians—having their needs met during their pilgrimage was not enough, no matter that the promise of a new homeland, a new life, and a new freedom lay at the end of the journey.

Prepared for the Battle:

For if the trumpet give an uncertain sound, who shall prepare himself to the battle? [1 Corinthians 14:8]

When Jesus said, "I go to prepare a place for you," He was reminding us that this world is not our home. We have a far better dwelling place awaiting us at the end of our earthly sojourning. "Let us go forth therefore unto him [Jesus] without the camp, bearing his reproach. For here we have no continuing city, but we seek one to come" (Hebrews 13:13–14). Our city, our homeland, is an eternal kingdom—the kingdom of God. Our true citizenship is in Heaven.

But what does He mean when He tells us to "go forth therefore unto him without the camp, bearing his reproach?" The Greek word translated "camp" refers to *an encampment prepared for battle.* Our Lord left the camp to come to this world and bear His reproach—the reproach of the cross. He left His throne in His Father's house and bore that cross to a hill called Golgotha, Mount Calvary, giving us the only hope we have for our salvation. We remain outside the camp, our heavenly home, between the cross and Satan's domain, ready to do battle. Our mission is to deliver the message of hope and salvation to a lost and dying world. Our immediate goal is to "go forth therefore unto him without the camp, bearing his reproach."

While we remain outside the camp, we are torn between two competing desires: the first, of course, is not just a desire but a command—that is to take up the cross, or as Hebrews 13 says, to bear the reproach that Christ bore for us, to go out from the camp and fight a good fight against the wiles of the devil. In so doing, as Paul instructs the man of God, we must "fight the good fight of faith, [and] lay hold on eternal life, whereunto thou art also called, and hast professed a good profession *before many witnesses*" (1 Timothy 6:12). In context, Timothy was the specific "man of God" referred to, and certainly his profession was before many witnesses, but the same declaration applies to every believer. When we profess to being followers of Christ, we are given the mandate to be witnesses to both the world and the Church, witnesses of our own profession of faith in Christ and sharing the message of the cross with others.

The second competing desire is to be with Christ. We are to go forth "unto him." In Matthew 28:20, Jesus assured His disciples that as they went out to the nations to spread the gospel, "Lo, I am with you alway, even unto the end of the world." But that goal can't be fully realized until our warfare on Earth is complete. Remember that Jesus said, "And if I go and prepare a place for you, I will come again, and receive you unto myself; that where I am, there ye may be also." In this regard, it is evident that Christ is just as anxious to be with us as we are with Him. In John 14:18, He said, "I will not leave you comfortless: I will come to you."

Let's consider our relationship and witness to our fellow believers, especially considering the fact that we are living in the most evil times of our lives, facing the war of all wars, mainly between the world, the flesh, and the devil. These are times when the governments of men are determined to destroy every effort to disseminate the

17

gospel of our salvation and the very existence of the family of God—the Bride of our Lord Jesus Christ.

Paul wrote to the troubled Thessalonian believers: "Ye are all the children of light, and the children of the day: we are not of the night, nor of darkness. Therefore let us not sleep, as do others; but let us watch and be sober. For they that sleep sleep in the night; and they that be drunken are drunken in the night. But let us, who are of the day, be sober, putting on the breastplate of faith and love; and for an helmet, the hope of salvation. For God hath not appointed us to wrath, but to obtain salvation by our Lord Jesus Christ, Who died for us, that whether we wake or sleep, we should live together with him. Wherefore *comfort yourselves together*, and *edify one another*, even as also you do" (1 Thessalonians 4:5–11).

The Greek word translated as "edify" literally means *be a house-builder*. The house we are to build is the household of God. There are two ways we build the household of God. We begin by winning unbelievers to our Lord Jesus Christ just as the early church did in the book of Acts. Being filled with the Holy Spirit the Church marched to His drumbeat and "the Lord added to the church daily such as should be saved" (Acts 2:47). There is nothing more important than the saving of a lost soul—neither food nor drink nor a roof over your head! The reasons Christ came to this earth were to save sinners: "For the Son of man is come to seek and to save that which was lost" (Luke 19:10), and to establish His Lordship over every creature: "For to this end [or for this purpose] Christ both died, and rose, and revived, that he might be Lord both of the dead and living" (Romans 14:9).

Once we have placed ourselves under His Lordship He becomes the Captain of our salvation: "For it became him, for whom are all things, and by whom are all things, *in bringing many sons unto glory*, to make the captain of their salvation perfect through sufferings [the suffering of the cross]" (Hebrews 2:10). Notice that Christ is the One who created all things by and for Himself for the purpose of "bringing many sons unto glory." Once we yield ourselves to Him, we are instructed to take up where He left off. After His resurrection, Jesus told His disciples, "As my Father hath sent me, even so send I you" (John 20:21).

After Jesus had washed His disciples' feet, He told Peter, "For *I have given you an example*, that ye should *do as I have done* to you. Verily, verily, I say unto you, The servant is not greater than his Lord; neither he that is sent greater than he that sent him. If ye know these things, happy are ye if ye *do them*" (John 13:15–17). It is a lesson for every believer who calls Jesus Lord. He said at that same event, "Ye call me Master and Lord: and ye say well; for so I am" (13).

Christ is both our example and our Lord. If we fail to follow the leadership of the Captain of our salvation, our battles with sin and the devil are lost at the expense of those who are in need of the hope of glory. Since Christ gave His life in order to bring "many sons unto glory," then we must give our lives to that same cause.

Our first desire then is to build the household of God. The second desire is that we yearn to go home. We're homesick for Heaven! Paul reminds us that in the here and now we "groan within ourselves, waiting for the adoption, to wit, the redemption of our body. For we are

19

saved by hope" (Romans 8:23–24). Our mandate is to take up the cross and follow Jesus into the fray, but the final victory will take place on the day of redemption. Just as the children of God have suffered down through the ages, sometimes with patience and sometimes with doubt, Paul continues his reminder in verse 25, "But if we hope for that we see not, then do we *with patience* wait for it."

And what is it that we hope for"? In verses 16–18, Paul gives us the assurance that "we are the children of God: And if children, then heirs; heirs of God, and joint-heirs with Christ; if so be that we suffer with him, that we may be also glorified together. For I reckon that the sufferings of this present time are not worthy to be compared with the glory which shall be revealed in us."

What then must we do at this present time? We are to "run with patience the race that is set before us, Looking unto Jesus the author and finisher of our faith; who for the joy that was set before him endured the cross, despising the shame, and is set down at the right hand of the throne of God" (Hebrews 12:1–2), and how do we run this race? Peter tell us in 1 Peter 4:1–2, "Forasmuch then as Christ hath suffered for us in the flesh, arm yourselves likewise with the same mind: for he that hath suffered in the flesh hath ceased from sin; That he no longer should live the rest of his time in the flesh to the lusts of men, but to the will of God."

Israel was weak in warfare. It would be a stretch to say that they knew how to fight a good fight of faith as they left the camp and faced the wilderness. Numbers 21:4–5 gives this account of Israel's sojourn: "And they journeyed from Mount Hor by the way of the Red Sea, to compass the land of Edom: and the soul of the people was much discouraged because of *the way*. And the people spake against God, and against Moses, Wherefore have ye brought us up out of Egypt to die in the wilderness? For there is no bread, neither is there any water; and our soul loatheth this light bread."

Remember that the "light bread" the Israelites complained about, saying they loathed or hated it, represented our Lord Jesus Christ. That was the bread that sustained their lives by the grace of Almighty God. Without it they would have perished in the wilderness of their own making, just as it is with the church today. In John 6:32–33, Jesus told those who had experienced the feeding of the five thousand, "Verily, verily, I say unto you, Moses gave you not that bread from heaven; but my Father giveth you the true bread from heaven. For the bread of God is he which cometh down from heaven, and gave life unto the world."

Israel had experienced miracle after miracle at the hand of God, but they had not learned to obey the Lord and to follow His leading. They had a different time schedule in mind, and their time was not in sync with God's time. God's chosen people had failed to allow God His sovereign place as the Lord of their lives. When that happens, even today, people leave themselves open to judgment. The Hebrew people had failed to keep their eyes, their minds, and their hearts fixed on that ultimate goal—the Promised Land.

The Apostle Paul said in Philippians 3:14–17, "I press toward the mark for the prize of the high calling of God in Christ Jesus. Let us therefore, as many as be perfect, be thus minded: and if in any thing ye be otherwise minded, God shall reveal even this unto you. Nevertheless, whereto we have already attained, let us walk by the same rule, let us mind the same thing. Brethren, be followers together of me, and mark them which walk so as ye have us for an example." Then in verse 18, he warns that "many walk, of whom I have told you often, and now tell you even weeping, that they are the enemies of the cross of Christ."

That's what we are facing in today's churches, and there are many who preach another gospel than that which Paul preached! It's the difference between the trumpeter that gives a clear sound of the trumpet and the one whose sound is uncertain. When an ambulance sounds its siren, you know that you must get out of its way, but if the driver were to lean out the window and yell, "beep, beep," there would probably be an accident in the making! So it would be if you were commanding an army to charge the enemy, but the trumpeter sounded "retreat" instead. Wouldn't it make you wonder who your enemy is?

The people of Israel fit that category in their relationship with God. They actually rejected the Bread from Heaven—a type of the Lord Jesus Christ. John reminds us of the words of Jesus in John 6:47–51: "Verily, verily, I say unto you, He that believeth on me hath everlasting life. I am that bread of life. Your fathers did eat manna in the wilderness, and are dead. This is the bread which cometh down from heaven, that a man may eat thereof, and not die. *I am the living bread which came down from heaven*: if any man eat of this bread, he shall live forever: and the bread that I will give is my flesh, which I will give for the life of the world."

22

Israel soon learned what it meant to rebel against Almighty God. "And the Lord sent fiery serpents among the people, and they bit the people; and much people of Israel died" (Numbers 21:6). By rejecting the bread sent down from Heaven, they were rejecting the Gift of God—the type of Christ Himself. The children of Israel needed the manna to give them life, just as we need Christ to give us everlasting life.

But they did have a way out. They did not need to die by the serpent's bite. Just as we today must follow the way of the cross—the sacrificial Lamb of God—in order to live and not die, they, too, were required to follow the way of the cross. That cross was represented by a brass serpent mounted on a pole. "And the Lord said unto Moses, Make thee a fiery serpent, and set it upon a pole: and it shall come to pass, that every one that is bitten, when he looketh upon it, shall live. And Moses made a serpent of brass, and put it upon a pole, and it came to pass, that if a serpent had bitten any man, when he beheld the serpent of brass, he lived" (Numbers 21:8–9).

Jesus said that the experience of the serpents in the wilderness was given as a picture of what was to happen to Him on Calvary's cross. He told Nicodemus in John 3:14–15, "And as Moses lifted up the serpent in the wilderness, even so must the Son of man be lifted up: That whosoever believeth in him should not perish, but have eternal life." The serpent of brass was a picture of Christ on the cross. There is not a doubt in my mind that the pole that Moses held high was a cross with a brass serpent nailed to it. Those who looked to the figure were saved from death, and those who look to Jesus as the Author and Finisher of their faith are saved from the second death described in the Book of Revelation.

Hebrews 12:1–2 tells us to fix our eyes on Jesus. "Wherefore seeing we also are compassed about by a cloud of witnesses, let us lay aside every weight, and the sin which doth so easily beset us, and let us run with patience the race that is set before us, *Looking unto Jesus* the author and finisher of our faith; who for the joy that was set before him endured the cross, despising the shame, and is set down at the right hand of the throne of God."

When Jesus said, "I am the way," He meant just that. It may seem that we can have a thousand ways to go, but it boils down to just two—life and death—and it is left to us to choose our way. On the one hand, Proverbs 14:12 warns us: "There is a way that seemeth right unto a man, but the end thereof are the ways of death." That's what Paul referred to in Philippians 3:18–19: "For many walk, of whom I have told you often, and now tell you even weeping, that they are the enemies of the cross of Christ: Whose end is destruction, whose God is their belly, and whose glory is in their shame, who mind earthly things."

We are at war with the enemy of the cross, but the Psalmist gave us a rallying cry: "Thou hast given a banner to them that fear thee, that it may be displayed because of the truth" (Psalm 60:4). That banner for us is the banner of the cross. Paul reminds us in Romans 13:12, "The night is far spent, the day is at hand: let us therefore cast off the works of darkness, and let us put on the armour of light."

The way of the cross is the only way to Heaven, and that cross belongs to our Lord Jesus Christ. If we want to inherit eternal life, we must join Him in the way because He *is* the way. The banner we carry is the cross of Christ.

Jesus said that "whosoever doth not bear his cross, and come after me, cannot be my disciple" (Luke 14:27). If we don't follow the way of the cross, then we simply have never found it!

Just as the young man came running down the road to catch up with the Master and fell on his knees, many hurry down the aisle at invitation time at the local church or a mass evangelistic rally—sometimes falling on their knees as the young ruler did—but when they get to the preacher they are often told they must "accept Christ as their Savior" (an expression that never appears in the Bible), but they are rarely told they must take up the cross and follow Him. At that point, they must hang their head and walk away because they have not chosen the way of the cross.

An Army of Sheep:

All ye shall be offended [Greek: entrapped]
because of me this night: for it is written, I
will smite the shepherd, and the sheep of the
flock shall be scattered abroad. But after I
am risen again, I will go before you . . . .
[Matthew 26:31–32]

Jesus said, "My sheep hear my voice, and I know them, and *they follow me*; And I give unto them eternal life; and they shall never perish, neither shall any pluck them out of my hand" (John 10:27–28). How ironic that the verse people claim as the assurance that they will live forever sets as a required standard that they must follow Him. Think about this, Jesus said, "I am the good shepherd: the good shepherd giveth his life for the sheep" (10:11). If the King of kings and Lord of lords was not only willing to accomplish what He did for us but left His throne in Heaven to suffer, bleed and die for you and me, how can we do less for Him?

I once sat in an adult Sunday School class in which this thought was expressed. I looked across the table at a man who had a look of amazement on his face. "I could never do that!" he said. "I don't think I would ever be willing to die for Christ! I think it's enough that I accepted Him as my Savior!" The fact is, that man did not know Christ. As is often the case, it was as though he thought he was doing Christ a favor by finding Him acceptable.

The man missed the point. No one had said that he had to die for Christ, but that he had to give the owner-

26

ship of his life to Christ. Paul said in Romans 6:6–11, "Knowing this, that our old man is crucified with him, that the body of sin might be destroyed, that henceforth we should not serve sin. For he that is dead is freed from sin. Now if we be dead with Christ, we believe that we shall also live with him: Knowing that Christ being raised from the dead dieth no more; death hath no more dominion over him. For in that he died, he died unto sin [our sin] once: but in that he liveth, he liveth unto God. Likewise reckon ye also to be dead indeed unto sin, but alive unto God through Jesus Christ our Lord."

I spent a great summer session at Wheaton College in 1960, and the school's motto has been permanently fixed in my mind: "For Christ and His Kingdom." That is the motto that every believer must apply to his or her life. In Matthew 10:38, Jesus said, "He that taketh not his cross, and followeth after me, is not worthy of me. He that findeth his life shall lose it: and he that loseth his life *for my sake* shall find it" (10:38–39). But if we are not *willing* to go so far as to die in the name of Jesus Christ, we fall far short of belonging to Him. Perhaps that's what He meant when He said, "So the last shall be first, and the first last: for many be called, but few chosen" (Matthew 20:16).

When Jesus called to each of his potential disciples, the Scripture says that they dropped everything and followed Him. So typical were the experiences of Simon Peter, Andrew, James, and John in Mark 1:16–20: "Now as he [Jesus] walked by the sea of Galilee, he saw Simon and Andrew his brother casting a net into the sea: for they were fishers. And Jesus said unto them, Come ye after me and I will make you to become fishers of men. And straightway [*immediately*] they *forsook their nets, and followed him.* And when he had gone a little further thence, he saw James the son of Zebedee, and John his brother, who also were in the ship mending their nets. And straightway he called them: and *they left their father Zebedee in the ship with the hired servants, and went after him.*"

In John 1:35–37, we have this account: "Again the next day after John [the Baptist] stood, and two of his [John's] disciples; And looking upon Jesus as he walked, he saith, Behold the Lamb of God! And the two disciples heard him speak, and *they followed Jesus.*" Verse 43 tells us that the next day "Jesus would go forth into Galilee, and findeth Philip, and saith unto him, *Follow me.*" Not only did Philip follow Jesus without hesitating, but he went after Nathaniel and brought him to Jesus. In fact, after Christ ascended to His Father, Philip continued to bring people to Christ as an evangelist. Every man who was called to follow Christ did so without any concern for themselves. They all took up the cross and followed Him—even to the forfeiture of their lives!

It is fitting that the Gospel of John closes with the Lord's admonition to Peter to feed His sheep. Then Jesus told Peter about his own impending crucifixion "signifying by what death he should glorify God. And when he had spoken this, he saith unto him, *Follow me.* Then Peter, turning about, seeth the disciple whom Jesus loved *following*" (John 21:19–20). All of the apostles gave their lives for the cause of Christ, and down through the ages, many thousands of His followers have willingly died in His service. But one must recognize the fact that you can't be a follower of Christ if you don't follow Him, and the way to follow Him is the way of the cross!

Remember this. While so many preachers today talk about how easy it is to be a Christian, Romans 8:16–18 paints a different picture: "The Spirit [Himself] beareth witness with our spirit, that we are the children of God: And if children, then heirs; heirs of God, and joint-heirs with Christ; *if so be that we suffer with him*, that we may also be glorified together. For I reckon that the sufferings of this present time are not worthy to be compared with the glory which shall be revealed in us."

No religious group has been more persecuted and tormented from its inception than the Christian and Jewish communities of believers. Millions of Christians have been slain just for being Christians, as were millions of Jews during World War II and throughout the history of the Jews. It is against the law in practically every Islamic country to be a Christian. American Christians don't have any concept of what is going on in the rest of the world, and frankly, we are spoiled by our possessions and worldly activities. We simply have no concept of Biblical separation and commitment to Jesus Christ. When we do come to the realization of what God expects of us, and only then, will we discover what it really means to be a true Christian, a true follower of Christ. It will require sacrifice, obedience, and holy living. That's why our Lord said that "many be called, but few chosen!"

Does a man have to die for Christ? No. But a man must live for Christ, and if in the process of living for Christ He must surrender his life, then he has fulfilled the highest calling of God and has won a crown of righteousness! Why is it that a young man will join the military and willingly go off to war to defend our country? He may lose his limbs or his sight or even his life, and those who know what he did rightly call him a hero. But the same young man, or those whom he left behind, would never consider going off to war against the world and the devil to defend and proclaim the saving grace of God through Jesus Christ our Lord. On the one hand, he was willing to take up the flag we call *Old Glory* and follow it to the death, but perhaps he refused to take up the banner of the cross and follow Christ into *His Glory* and everlasting life!

There is another old hymn I remember so well that no longer appears in some hymn books today, perhaps because it contains a message that no one wants to hear in these days of backsliding and apostasy. The first verse says, "I must needs go home by the way of the cross, there's no other way but this. I shall ne'er get sight of the gates of light, if the way of the cross I miss." If you've never considered the way of the cross, there's no better time than now to pick up that banner and follow the Master into the battlefield.

The First World War was dubbed "the war to end all wars," but sad to say, that was not the case. In my own lifetime, since that war to end all wars, our country has struggled through five wars, as well as several "minor skirmishes," and the struggles still continue. There will never be peace in this world, but the hope that our Lord has given is that, at the end of the way of the cross, there will be no more crosses to bear and no more battles to fight. When the last battle has been won, there will be the glory of final peace that will go on for eternity when this world has passed away and a new Heaven and new Earth appear, for He has said, "He maketh wars to cease unto the end of the earth" (Psalm 46:9a).

The Way of Truth:

I have chosen the way of truth:
thy judgments have I laid before
me. **[Psalm 119:30]**

In John 14:6, Jesus also said that He is *the Truth*. When Jesus was brought before Pilate, the procurator of Judaea, under whose authority Christ was to be judged, Jesus said, "Thou sayest that I am a king. To this end was I born, and for this cause came I into the world, that I should bear witness unto the truth. Every one that is of *the truth* heareth *my* voice" (John 18:37). It was a unique way for Christ to say, "If you believe in truth, you believe in me, because I *am* the Truth."

Pilate didn't grasp the meaning of His words. His response was simply, "What is truth?" because he was not "of the truth." He could hear Him speak, but he couldn't hear His voice. That may sound a little confusing, but on many occasions Jesus said, "Let him that hath ears to hear, let him hear." It was His challenge to his "listeners" to pay close attention. Today we might say, "Don't just let this go in one ear and out the other." Others might say, "Let me knock some sense into your head." Pilate would have done well to pay heed to what David said in Psalm 95:7–8: "For he is our God; and we are the people of his pasture, and the sheep of his hand. To day if ye will hear his voice, Harden not your heart, as in the provocation, and as in the day of temptation in the wilderness."

We, too, must pay heed. The writer of Hebrews placed a limit upon the days that men are allowed to respond to that truth. In Hebrews 4:7, he said, "Again,

31

he limiteth a certain day, saying in David, Today if ye
will hear his voice, harden not your hearts." In verse 11
he adds, "Let us labour therefore to enter into that rest
[eternal rest with Christ], lest any man fall after the same
example of unbelief."

God warned in Genesis 6:3, "My Spirit shall not always strive with man." In that same chapter, we are told,
"And God saw that the wickedness of man was great in
the earth, and that every imagination of the thoughts of
his heart was only evil continually. And it repented the
Lord that he had made man on the earth, and it grieved
him at his heart. And the Lord said, I will destroy man
whom I have created from the face of the earth; both
man, and beast, and the creeping thing, and the fowls
of the air; for it repenteth me that I have made them"
(Genesis 6:5–7). Verse 8 reminds us that God is still a
gracious God, and the Scripture tells us that "Noah found
grace in the eyes of the Lord."

There are those who have convinced themselves that
God would never do such a thing again. "After all," they
will say, "Isn't that why we have rainbows to remind us
that God will never destroy man again?" I have to tell
such people that God made no such promise. He said He
would never destroy mankind again by a flood. There is
coming a judgment that is far worse than a flood. What is
coming is beyond human imagination, even though it is
vividly described in the book of Revelation. Luke 17:26–
27 warns, "And as it was in the days of Noe [Noah], so
shall it be also in the days of the Son of man. They did
eat, they drank, they married wives, they were given in
marriage, until the day that Noe entered into the ark, and
the flood came and destroyed them all."

The same things that happened in Noah's day happened in Sodom and Gomorrha, but in those two cities God rained fire down upon them! This is a truth that few people take to heart. While we see films and read books everywhere that Christ's return is imminent and that He will judge the world, people still behave as though they have no fear or reverence for God and what God has said He will do.

In this context, let me repeat what Jesus said in John 10:27–28, "My sheep *hear my voice*, and I know them, and they follow me: And I give unto them eternal life; and they shall never perish, neither shall any man pluck them out of my hand." The evidence that anyone has actually *heard* His voice is that *he follows Him*. He recognizes the Truth. As a result, that person has been given eternal life, guaranteed by the Lord Jesus Himself!

Jesus was telling Pilate to listen up, but the Lord knew that Pilate was not willing to listen. Pilate had ears to hear but didn't hear what Jesus was saying. He heard only the words he wanted to hear, but he was not open to the truth. He asked Jesus if He were really a king. Jesus told him, "Yes, I am. That is the reason I was born. That's why I came into the world—so I could bear witness of myself. I am the truth, and those who are mine will hear and believe what I have to say." Pilate was neither ready nor willing to hear the Truth.

Our Lord gave a clear answer even before Pilate asked the question, "What is truth?" It was when He told His disciples that He would leave them and return to His Father's house as He contemplated the very reason for the confrontation He was to have with Pilate. After telling the disciples of His coming departure, He said, "I am *the way*, *the truth*, and *the life*. No man cometh unto the Father, but by me" (John 14:6).

It's difficult to understand a concept like truth embodied as a person. In John 8:31–36, Jesus was being questioned by the Pharisees. Some of the Jews who heard the discussion believed His word, and He said to them, "If ye continue in my word, then ye are my disciples indeed; And ye shall know the truth, and the truth shall make you free." Being Jews under the Law of Moses, they responded, "We be Abraham's seed, and were never in bondage to any man: how sayest thou, Ye shall be made free?"

Evidently they had forgotten Israel's history and the several times the people of Abraham's seed had been taken into captivity. At any rate, their response was far removed from the truth. "Jesus answered them, Verily, verily, I say unto you, Whosoever committeth sin is the servant of sin. And the servant abideth not in the house for ever: but the Son abideth ever. If *the Son* therefore shall make you free, ye shall be free indeed."

In Colossians 3:9–10, Paul admonishes us, "Lie not one to another, seeing that ye have put off the old man with his deeds; And have put on the new man, which is renewed in knowledge after the image of him that created him." What we must keep in mind is that when we confess Christ as our Lord, we must emulate Him in everything we do and say. We are no longer the person we used to be—the old man. We have become what God wants us to be—a new man—a man who is renewed, made over again, in our knowledge that we have put on the "image of him that created" us through the indwelling presence of the Holy Spirit. Christ is now in us to guide us into the truth, "Christ is all, and in all" (Colossians 3:11).

Do you see the clarification the Lord was making? In essence, He said, "Ye shall know the truth, and the *truth* shall make you free. Let me repeat that, If the *Son* shall make you free, ye shall be free indeed." In other words it was the same as saying, "I am the truth, and I shall make you free indeed."

We are told in John 1:14 that "the Word was made flesh, and dwelt among us, (and we beheld his glory, the glory as of the only begotten of the Father,) full of grace and truth," and in verse 17, John the Baptist said, "For the law was given by Moses, but grace and truth came by Jesus Christ." It is obvious that the answer to Pilate's question "What is truth?" is *Jesus Christ*. Christ is the very embodiment of truth. The world may reject Him, but the world is engulfed in lies. To deny Christ is to deny the truth. In his first epistle John said, "Who is a liar but he that denieth that Jesus is the Christ? He is antichrist, that denieth the Father and the Son" (1 John 2:22).

John reported the words of Christ when he was confronted by the Pharisees regarding the author of lies and those who believe his lies in John 8:42–47: "If God were your Father, ye would love me: for I proceeded forth and came from God; neither came I of myself, but he that sent me. Why do ye not understand my speech? Even because ye cannot hear my word. Ye are of your father the devil, and the lusts of your father ye will do. He was a murderer from the beginning [a reference to the Garden of Eden], and abode not in the truth, because there is no truth in him. When he speaketh a lie, he speaketh of his own: for he is a liar and the father of it. And because I tell you the truth, ye believe me not. Which of you convinceth [*admonishes* or *convicts*] me of sin? And if I say the truth, why do ye not believe me? He that is of God heareth God's words: ye therefore hear them not, because ye are not of God."

Then in verses 54–55, Jesus pegs the Pharisees for what they are: "If I honour myself, my honour is nothing: it is my Father that honoureth me; of whom ye say, that he is your God: Yet ye have not known him; but I know him: and if I should say, I know him not, I shall be *a liar like unto you*: but I know him, and keep his saying."

While Jesus was speaking directly to the Pharisees, what He said applies to everyone in the world today. There are only two kinds of people in the world: those who believe the truth that rests in the Lord Jesus Christ, thereby gaining eternal life, and those who believe the devil—the worst mass-murderer of all—who, because of his lies, led Adam and Eve to rebel against God, bringing death upon all mankind. Those who reject the Truth will die in their sins, eternally separated from God and abandoned to the lake of fire as described in Revelation 20:15.

I once had a conversation with a young man who told me that he didn't need Jesus Christ because he wasn't a sinner. I asked him, "Do you mean that you have never done anything wrong? You have never lied, or taken something that didn't belong to you? Have you never had lustful thoughts about a woman? Have you never taken the name of the Lord in vain?" I paused for his answer.

"Everyone has done those things. It's just a natural part of life." That was about the only way he could answer because he had done all of those things as a matter of habit.

"That's what I'm talking about," I said. Then I pointed out what the Scriptures teach about sin. What I told him is as true for everyone else as it was for him. In Romans 3:10–12, Paul quoted Psalm 14 when he said, "As it is written, There is none righteous, no, not one: There is none that understandeth, there is none that seeketh after [meaning: *to search out*, *investigate*, or *worship*] God. They are all gone out of the way, they are together become unprofitable; there is none that doeth good, no, not one."

Jesus said in John 6:44, "No man can come to me, except the Father which hath sent me draw him: and I will raise him up at the last day." In other words, you must hear the voice of God when He speaks to your heart. When you do, you will receive everlasting life, and you will be lifted up bodily (howbeit, a new body) to Heaven at the end of this age.

Romans 3:23 tells us that "*all* have sinned and come short of the glory of God," and Romans 6:23 makes it clear that "the wages of sin is death; but the gift of God is eternal life through Jesus Christ our Lord."

The young man with whom I spoke was a perfect example of what John said in 1 John 1:8, "If we say we have no sin, we deceive ourselves, and *the truth* is not in us." Without the truth being in us, we would all be destined to spend eternity in the lake of fire, forever separated from God and all hope of redemption.

37

The Holy Spirit moved John to declare the truth as he saw it expressed in Christ in no uncertain terms. In his first epistle, John said, "And *we know* that the Son of God is come, and hath given us an *understanding* [the same understanding the Psalmist spoke about in Psalm 14], that we may *know him that is true*, and we are *in him that is true*, even *in his Son Jesus Christ*. This is the true God, and eternal life" (1 John 5:20).

Truth as a description for Jesus Christ is made clear in 2 John 1–4: "The elder unto the elect lady and her children, whom I love in the truth: and not I only, but also all they that have known the truth; For the truth's sake, which dwelleth in us, and shall be with us for ever. Grace be with you, mercy, and peace, from God the Father, and from the Lord Jesus Christ, the Son of the Father, in truth and love. I rejoiced greatly that I found of thy children walking in truth, as we have received a commandment from the Father."

John refers to the Truth that dwells in us and that the Truth shall be with us forever. Paul tells us in Romans 8:9 that the Spirit of Christ dwells in us. In verse 10 he says, "And if Christ be in you, the body is dead because of sin; but the Spirit is life because of righteousness." The Lord Jesus Christ Himself refers to the Holy Spirit as the Spirit of truth in John 14:17, 15:26, and 16:13. So when John tells us that the truth dwells in us and shall be with us forever, he is referring to the indwelling presence of the Spirit of Christ in every believer. Jesus said that the Holy Spirit will "abide with you for ever; even the Spirit of truth."

The answer to Pilate's question, "What is truth," is, as we have seen, given by Christ in John 14:6, "*I* am the way, the truth, and the life."

Our hope of eternal redemption rests in one great truth, the truth that is reflected in the words of Jesus to Martha in John 11:25–26, "I am the resurrection, and the life: he that believeth in me, though he were dead, yet shall he live; And whosoever liveth and believeth in me shall never die. Believeth thou this?"

The Way of Life:

When Christ, who is our life, shall
appear, then shall ye also appear
with him in glory. [Colossians 3:4]

What is the origin of life? There are many people, especially among so-called scientists who think life came from the sea, but they still haven't explained its origin. No one on Earth can create life. It's an unexplainable entity in all "living" organisms. You can't see or touch it. The only evidence that it exists is that the creatures on Earth possess it! The simple truth is that the mind of the most highly educated, most sophisticated man or woman on Earth with the highest possible IQ has no more intelligence than the smallest flea compared to the mind of Almighty God! That simple truth is established by the fact that "the natural man receiveth not [or *cannot accept*] the things of the Spirit of God: for they are foolishness unto him: neither can he know them, because they are spiritually discerned" (1 Corinthians 2:14). In other words, he's not smart enough to begin to comprehend the most basic of all truth—that God exists and created all things for His good pleasure!

The Bible explains what life is and what its source is, but ungodly people will never accept the truth about life. Where man is concerned, he had no life at all until Almighty God breathed it into him. Genesis 1:26 reports that "God said, Let us make man in our image, after our likeness."

Then in Genesis 2:7, "the Lord God formed man of the dust of the ground, and breathed into his nostrils the breath of life; and man became a living soul." Sad to say, man lost that image and likeness of God when he chose to disobey the one command that God had given him. Sin reduced the spiritual life that God had given him to a carnal existence destined to die. The only way to recover that loss was to provide a means of spiritually reentering the body of man. That came by way of the Holy Spirit through the sacrifice of Christ and His shed blood on the cross.

So let's consider the third link between the three elements of who Jesus is—the Way, the Truth and *the Life*. In John 10:10, Jesus said, "I am come that they might have life, and that they might have it more abundantly." Contrary to what some greedy preachers in today's churches teach, abundant life has nothing to do with the riches of this world. It has to do with the abundance of God's mercy toward us.

Paul clarifies it in Ephesians 2:4–7: "But God, who is rich [*abundant*] in mercy, for his great love wherewith he loved us, Even when we were dead in sins, hath quickened us [*brought us to life*] together with Christ, (by grace ye are saved;) And hath raised us up together, and made us sit together in heavenly places in Christ Jesus: That in *the ages to come* he might shew the exceeding riches of his grace in his kindness toward us through Christ Jesus."

Notice that verse 5 tells us our abundant life is *with Christ*, verse 6 that it is *in Christ*, and verse 7 that it is *through Christ*. Why? Because Christ *is* the richness, or abundance, of our life. It is expressed by His mercy. He is *the* life! But we must keep in mind that all three phrases point to the cross. In Galatians 2:20, Paul said,

41

"I am crucified *with Christ*: nevertheless *I live*; yet not I, but *Christ liveth in me*: and the life which I now live in the flesh I live by the faith of the Son of God, who loved me and gave himself for me."

In 1 John 4:13 we are told, "Hereby know we that we dwell *in him*, and he in us, because he hath given us of his Spirit." That's His mercy, His love, His grace! But it's only the beginning of His abundant life for us. Verse 7 tells us that Christ will supply the exceeding riches, our ultimate abundant life, in the *ages to come*—eternity! In verse 9 we are told, "In this was manifested the love of God toward us, because that God sent his only begotten Son into the world, that we might live *through him*."

Our life in Christ has nothing to do with money or any other worldly possession. In Matthew 6:19–21, Jesus exhorts us to "lay not up for yourselves treasures upon earth, where moth and rust doth corrupt, and where thieves break through and steal: But lay up for yourselves treasures in heaven, where neither moth nor rust doth corrupt, and where thieves do not break through nor steal: For where your treasure is there will your heart be also." And in verse 33, He says, "But seek ye *first* the kingdom of God, and *his righteousness*; and all these things [*this abundance*] shall be added unto you."

Your treasure in Heaven depends entirely with how you conduct your life in the here and now—what you do for the cause of Christ and not what you do for yourself. Keep in mind the account of the rich young ruler who thought that his keeping the ten commandments could somehow earn him a reward in Heaven. If not, surely the fact that he was a man of great means could make him worthy. But no! Only the cross of Christ was sufficient.

"Take up the cross," Jesus said, "and follow me." You see, it wasn't the righteousness of the rich man, nor was it his corrupted worldly wealth that mattered at all! It was the righteousness of God and the riches of His kingdom that mattered, and they could only come by way of the cross.

When I was a young college student, enrolled at the state university, I committed my life to Christ and knew that God was calling me to the ministry. I wanted to transfer to a Bible college, but I couldn't afford it. A neighbor heard about my plight and invited me to his house to discuss the matter. "Larry," he said, "I believe you are doing a good thing, and I want to help you. I am going to pay your way through Bible college." I thanked him profusely and praised the Lord. He laughed and said, "Well, perhaps the Lord will make room for me when he finds out what I am doing."

I shook my head and told him that I could not accept his gracious offer and added, "I don't want you to think that your doing such a thing will get you a step closer to Heaven. Only your confessing Christ as your Lord and Savior can do that."

He, too, shook his head and said, "Well, if you change your mind, you know where you can get what you need." It took me thirteen years to get my first degree, but the Lord made sure that I could work my way through a little at a time. I gradually picked up Bible classes at Wheaton College and Moody Bible Institute. My job required my transferring to different parts of the country, so I studied at several more Bible schools a few courses at a time.

The Lord was preparing me for a traveling ministry, and my wife and I have shared our ministry of evangelism and revival from coast to coast and border to border! It took a lot longer to get there, but the Lord knew all along how *He* would achieve it! We gave up our house and most of our belongings, traveled in a used vehicle with our three children, never asked for money, and the Lord has never failed to keep us safe and provide for our needs. After all, we traveled *with Christ* proclaiming the "peace that passes understanding," the "joy unspeakable and full of glory," and eternal life through His sacrifice on the cross! And we knew that everything we did rested entirely *in Christ* and that those things that really mattered for eternity were accomplished *through Christ*.

Life, the only life that matters, is the life Christ gives us when we place our faith in Him and allow Him to be the Lord of our lives. The fact remains that life without him is not life at all because "even when we were *dead in sins*, [God] hath *brought us to life* together with Christ."

My friend, those are the same words He speaks to you and me. The fact remains that "as in Adam all die, even so in Christ shall all be made alive" (1 Corinthians 15:22). To this Paul adds in Romans 6:23, "For the wages of sin is death; but the gift of God is eternal life through Jesus Christ our Lord."

As Jesus said in John 14:6, "I am the way, the truth, and the life: no man cometh unto the Father, but by me." It is the absolute *truth* that Jesus Christ *is the truth,* and He *is the way* to life everlasting because He *is the life*. As Peter said in Acts 4:12, "Neither is there salvation in any other: for there is none other name under heaven given among men, whereby we must be saved." Once again, you cannot trust in any religion, or no religion at all. Whether you are a Muslim, a Buddhist, a Hindu, an atheist, or any other cultist, a millionaire or a pauper, a Catholic, a Protestant, or a Jew, a king or the President of the United States, without Christ you will spend eternity in hell.

Our promise of life rests in what Christ told Martha in John 11:25–26, "I am the resurrection, and the life: he that believeth in me, though he were dead, yet shall he live: And whosoever liveth and believeth in me shall never die. Believeth thou this?"

I believe it, do you?

The Way of the Cross

**There's a way that was made for the faithful and brave
For it's oft filled with sorrow and loss,
But the end of the way is a glorious day,
And it's known as the Way of the Cross.**

—Larry D. Rudder—

He Called Him "My Master"

Ye call me Master and Lord: and ye say well; for so I am.

—John 13:13—

Meet for the Master's Use:

But in a great house there are not only vessels of gold and of silver, but also of wood and of earth; and some to honour, and some to dishonour. If a man therefore purge himself from these, he shall be a vessel unto honour, sanctified, and meet for the Master's use, and prepared unto every good work. **[2 Timothy 2:20–21]**

Christians tend to believe what they believe because it's what they've been taught. I was actually confronted by a fundamental minister once who declared that he didn't care what the Bible said because his church held a different view from the New Testament verses we were reading. On another occasion a young lady told me that she couldn't understand the Bible so she just had to accept what she was taught. I thought, *How sad! Why, my youngest son read and understood the Authorized Version of the Bible, J.R.R. Tolkien, and other such reading material when he was in grade school.* I'm afraid the young lady's view of the Bible was rooted in her unwillingness to "study to show herself approved unto God," or she was simply too lazy to read it for herself. And how many times I've heard people state their confidence in certain issues based on the fact that their pastors, or great preachers (and some not so great) in history have held those views. Some have trusted their knowledge of the Scriptures to the voices that pour from their radios and televisions. While some of those voices are true to the Word of God, many are not, and it isn't always easy to distinguish between the good and the bad. No one should ever surrender his or her reasoning and spiritual acumen to anyone else. In other words, you are solely responsible for your relationship with Christ and your depth of the knowledge His Word.

A correct understanding of God's Word requires a lot of prayer and a lot of work. The fact is that if we enter our studies with our minds made up about everything, we're not going to learn anything. We must *study* the Bible to discover truths that we might otherwise miss, and if we think we already know everything, then why study at all?

The fact is that we are all subject to our own abilities to reason things out. Sometimes we are right, and sometimes we are wrong. It's often because we don't spend the time in prayer and the study of God's Word, or listen to the still, small voice of the Holy Spirit who offers us the light of the Word, and we fail to turn the light on! I, for one, will never be satisfied with my knowledge of God's Word. After fifty-four plus years of Bible study and preaching, I'm constantly learning, and the more time and effort I put into my studies, the greater my understanding becomes—and the more surprises I find— especially when I discover that I was in the right ballpark but swinging at the wrong pitches. Yet, I will never reach the point when I am satisfied with what little I know. After all, John tells us that "there are also many other things which Jesus did, the which, if they should be written every one, I suppose that even the world could not contain the books that should be written" (John 21:25).

Among those verses of Scripture that I will repeat often in this book is 2 Timothy 2:15. If God's people fail to grasp the urgency in this verse, we will utterly fail the Lord. Paul said, "Study to shew thyself approved unto God, a workman that needeth not to be ashamed, rightly dividing [literally: *dissecting*] the word of truth."

If we discover something that seems to contradict what we have always believed, then we need to know why. Rather than simply accepting it or explaining it away, we need to work through it. So let's delve even deeper into the Word.

Who is Jesus Christ? What does He mean to you? What is your relationship, if any, to Him? As my wife, Jeanette, and I have traveled from coast to coast preaching and singing the message of the hope of salvation, an issue has often arisen among many Christian fundamentalists regarding the Lordship of Jesus Christ resulting in a deep division among evangelicals. Sounds ludicrous, doesn't it? I find it unconscionable that anyone would choose to fight and divide the Church over such an issue—but it's just those types of things that have divided the Church for centuries. Let me make my position clear. If you are a born-again Christian, Jesus Christ is your Lord. If Jesus Christ is not your Lord, you are not a born-again Christian. Clear enough?

It's no wonder that the Church is experiencing a great "falling away" from the Lord of glory in these last days when men want to accept Christ as their Savior—but not confess Him as their Lord! That, of course, is a denial of His lordship. Since Paul tells us that we must confess Jesus as Lord in order to be saved in Romans 10:9, where he said "if thou shalt confess with thy mouth Jesus as Lord, and shalt believe in thine heart that God hath raised him from the dead, thou shalt be saved," committing our lives

51

to Christ as our Lord is the beginning of our salvation experience. That commitment opens the door to Heaven and the throne of Almighty God. It is His lordship that authorizes His position as Savior.

The third chapter of John is probably cited more often among Christian believers than any other portion of Scripture. In fact, many unbelievers have memorized one particular verse—the focal point of that chapter, of all of John's Gospel, and perhaps of the entire Bible— John 3:16: "For God so loved the world, that he gave his only begotten Son, that whosoever believeth in him should not perish, but have everlasting life." But there are many more passages in John's Gospel that require our undivided attention.

The third chapter truly sheds light on the Lord Jesus Christ and our relationship with (or without) Him, and is perhaps the most often quoted section of the Bible used to lead unbelievers to faith in Him. It begins with the account of a man who walks in darkness but comes to the Light of life with the most important question a man could ask of God, but who never openly asks it. His name is Nicodemus, a Pharisee, a ruler of the Jews, and member of the court of seventy elders known as the Sanhedrin Council. "The same came to Jesus *by night*, and said unto him, Rabbi [*my Master*], we know that thou art a teacher come from God: for no man can do these miracles that thou doest, except God be with him" (John 3:2).

Nicodemus' recognition of who Jesus was went beyond the norm for a man of his position and power. In darkness, he called out to Him, "Rabbi [Greek, from the Hebrew, *Rhabbi*, meaning: *my Master*], we know that thou art a teacher come from God: for no man can do these miracles that thou doest, except God be with him."

First, note that Nicodemus called Jesus, "my Master." The term used was one of great honor. There is no place in the New Testament that refers to Jesus as being made a Jewish rabbi, but He was indeed recognized as *the* Master as He dealt with those who sought after Him. In verse 10, Jesus said of Nicodemus, "Art thou a master [Greek *didaskalos* meaning: *instructor* or *teacher*] of Israel, and knowest not these things?" So when Nicodemus said, "my Master," he was calling Jesus the *Master of teachers.*" It was a unique statement expressing his confidence in who Jesus really was. At the same time, when Jesus called Nicodemus a master, He clarified the subordinate position that the man held—subordinate to the Master of teachers.

Jesus is the only person in the Bible who is called by this title except John the Baptist, who on one occasion was inappropriately called Rabbi by his own disciples when they asked him about Jesus in John 3:26, "And they came unto John, and said unto him, Rabbi, he that was with thee beyond Jordan, to whom thou bearest witness, behold, the same baptizeth, and all men come to him."

In Matthew 23:6–10, Jesus warns the disciples *not* to be like the Pharisees. He reminded them that the Pharisees "love the uppermost rooms at feasts, and the chief seats in the synagogues. And greetings in the markets, and to be called of men, Rabbi, Rabbi. But be not ye called Rabbi: for one is your Master, even Christ; and all ye are brethren. And call no man your father upon the earth: for one is your Father, which is in heaven.

Neither be ye called masters: for one is your Master, even Christ."

With that exhortation from Jesus, John's disciples were wrong in calling John the Baptist Rabbi. Notice that Jesus emphasized His admonition by repeating it: "Don't be called rabbi or master because there is only one Master, and I am that Master."

Nicodemus made another remarkable confession: "*We know* that thou art a teacher *come from God*." From this statement, we might assume that all of the Sanhedrin Council knew who Jesus was but chose to reject Him. Remember what John said: "He came unto his own, and his own received him not" (John1:11).

The Pharisees were what we would call in today's world "the apostasy." These are people who know who Jesus Christ is but reject His authority in their lives. They deny His lordship. After all, those who know without a doubt that Jesus is the Son of God, the angels that fell, "believe and tremble" (James 2:19). These angels would legitimately be called apostate angels.

The Pharisees wanted that authority for themselves. Isn't that just like the apostates of today? They want to apply the authority of Almighty God to themselves. Notice that Nicodemus did not say, "We *think* thou art a teacher come from God," but rather that "we *know* thou art a teacher come from God." In other words, Nicodemus was confessing that Jesus came from Heaven—the abode of God—and admitting that the rest of the Sanhedrin believed it, too.

Think about it! Isn't that exactly what happened to Adam and Eve in the Garden of Eden? When the serpent persuaded Eve to eat the fruit of the tree of the knowledge of good and evil, he said, "God doth know that in the day ye eat thereof, then your eyes shall be opened, ye shall be as gods, knowing good and evil" (Genesis 3:5). In other words, he was telling her that God was deceiving her, trying to keep her under His power and authority, wanting to have all of the power in His hands. Satan convinced her that by denying God's authority, she would have it for herself. That's just what those who reject Christ today think: "Why should I give my life, my independence, my power to do what I want to do, to God. Let God run the lives of the weak and beggarly. I can handle myself, thank you." Of course, Adam and Eve brought death and chaos upon themselves and the rest of creation! What will happen to the "authority" of those who deny Christ as their Lord, their Master, when they die? Who will have all of the authority then? Jesus said, "Whosoever therefore shall confess me before men, him will I confess also before my Father which is in heaven. But whosoever shall deny me before men, him will I also deny before my Father which is in heaven" (Matthew 10:32–33). Take note that He said absolutely nothing about accepting Him as your Savior. In fact, of all the doctrines of the evangelical churches, that is one that is not mentioned anywhere in the Bible!

Anyone who truly believes that the Bible is the Word of God would have to take the Lord Jesus Christ at His word. He told His disciples, "Ye call me Master and Lord: and ye say well; for so I am" (John 13:13). Have you ever considered the ramifications of what that statement means for you? Do you call Jesus *Master and Lord*, or do you reject His authority as Adam and Eve did? If the latter is the case, are you willing to become a castaway? That is, in fact, what happened to Adam and Eve. They were cast out of the garden of Eden and were never allowed back.

Hebrews 10:38–39 gives this warning: "Now the just shall live by faith: But if any man draw back, my soul shall find no pleasure in him. But we are not of them who draw back [turn their backs] unto perdition [damnation]; but of them that believe to the saving of the soul." We are given a choice: Christ and His kingdom or the world and its eternal judgment. If we choose Christ, we place ourselves under His authority. He is our Lord. If we turn our backs on Him and reject His authority, then we face an eternal hell.

He Is Lord!

And why call ye me, Lord Lord, and do not the things which I say? [Luke 6:46]

Isn't it ironic that not only was the Edenic couple the first people on Earth and the first to be selected by God to care for His creation, but they were also the first apostates? They believed in God, but they chose to reject His authority. James 2:19 reminds us that "the devils also believe and tremble." They also defected from Christ, thinking they could rise above Him and His authority.

The Bible teaches that there will be a great defection from Christ (apostates) in the last days. This brings us back to 2 Thessalonians 2:3, "Let no man deceive you by any means: for that day [the day of the Lord—the time labeled by some people as the tribulation] shall not come except there come a falling away [Greek: *apostasia*] first, and that man of sin be revealed, the son of perdition." I believe we are living in that time-frame, the age of apostasy, in which the churches will be crowded with people who call themselves Christians, but who reject the lordship of Christ!

Never forget that it is our confession that Christ is Lord, our supreme and final authority, and our belief that He was raised from the dead so that He could be Lord both of the dead and the living that brings us to redemption: "For none of us liveth to himself, and no man dieth to himself. For whether we live, we live unto the Lord; and whether we die, we die unto the Lord: whether we live therefore, or die, we are the Lord's. For to this end

57

[*for this reason*] Christ both died, and rose, and revived, *that he might be Lord* both of the dead and living" (Romans 14:7–9).

First Corinthians 15:1–5 specifies this as the gospel of our salvation: "Moreover, brethren, I declare unto you the gospel, which also I preached unto you, which also ye have received, and wherein ye stand; By which also ye are saved, if ye keep in memory what I preached unto you, unless ye have believed in vain; For I delivered unto you first of all that which I also received, how that Christ died for our sins according to the Scriptures; And that he was buried, and that he rose again the third day according to the Scriptures; And that he was seen." This is the same gospel presented in Romans 14 that tells us that the reason for this gospel is so that Jesus Christ "might be Lord both of the dead and living!"

Adam and Eve rebelled against the Lord. Their rebellion resulted in the fall of God's creation and the fall of man to the bondage of sin and death. The Lord Jesus Christ chose to come to this earth in the form of a man to redeem man from his sins. In so doing, the Son of God, Lord of lords, and King of kings suffered extreme humiliation, pain, and death on a Roman cross, shedding His blood so that every man, woman, and child could be saved from everlasting punishment for their rebellion against the Lord of glory—even for those who think they are wiser than God. We are all given the choice to serve the Lord Jesus Christ, thereby winning eternal life, or to serve our own pitiful ambitions without Christ, thereby earning eternal damnation.

Just pause for a moment and think about it. If Christ created us, if God the Father declared Him to be God and

Lord of that creation, and if our life on earth and for all eternity depends upon Him, how can we not recognize the fact that He owns us—lock, stock, and barrel? He is our Lord, and He has the total authority to decide what He will or will not do with us.

Jesus told His disciples, "All power is given unto me in heaven and in earth" (Matthew 28:18). How much power is given to Christ? All of it! There is no power or authority in the entire realm of God that exceeds that of Christ. At the throne of Almighty God, Jesus has *all* of the power because *all* power is given to Him in Heaven. The earth is His to do with as He pleases because *all* power is given to Him in Earth. Who are we in all of God's creation to reject that authority, that power?

Yet there are still those who fight over this very issue. They deny the relevance of the Lordship of Christ to the salvation experience. They claim that it relegates our salvation to *our* works when just the opposite is true. Our salvation depends entirely upon *His* works. If that were not true, He could not be Lord at all! There is no "work" involved in our turning our lives over to Christ. God is the one who sets the rules, not we pitiful, lowly people. We think we know more than God. We think we can tell God what He may or may not require for our salvation or, for that matter, how we live our lives.

It is to the contrary of those who deny the necessity of our confession of His Lordship—it is a doctrine of *commitment to Christ*. If you are one who denies this Biblical truth, then ask yourself this question: According to Romans 14:9, why did Christ die, rise from the dead, and live again? If your answer is anything less than "so He might be *Lord* both of the dead and living," then you are less than honest with yourself and with Almighty God. You would simply deny that the Bible is the Word of God.

In this same passage, Romans 14:8, we are told that we belong to the Lord—"We are the Lord's." In 1 Corinthians 6:20, Paul explains why this is true, "For ye are bought with a price [the precious blood of Jesus Christ]: therefore glorify God in your body, and in your spirit, *which are God's*." He repeats the thought in 7:22–23: "For he that is called in the Lord, being a servant, is the Lord's freeman: likewise also he that is called, being free, is *Christ's servant*. Ye are bought with a price; be not ye servants of men." In Ephesians 1:13–14 we see that "ye were sealed with that holy Spirit of promise, Which is the earnest of our inheritance until the day of redemption of the purchased possession, unto the praise of his glory."

You see, the Gospel, which is our salvation, rests entirely upon who He is and how we relate to Him. The reason Christ died, was buried, and rose again was to establish for us the fact that He is our Lord! Without that Lordship, Christ does not have the power or authority to save us from sin and redeem us to Himself! By rejecting His Lordship, we deny Him that authority.

Romans 10:9–10 informs us "that if thou shalt confess with thy mouth Jesus as Lord [the literal translation], and shalt believe in thine heart that God hath raised him from the dead, thou shalt be saved. For with the heart man believeth unto righteousness; and with the mouth confession is made *unto salvation*."

Since Jesus said in Matthew 10:32, "Whosoever therefore shall confess me before men, him will I confess also before my Father which is in heaven. But whosoever shall deny me before men, him will I deny before my Father which is in heaven," what is it that we must confess? *Jesus Christ is Lord!* But verbal expressions alone aren't enough. In this same chapter, Jesus explains Himself: "He that loveth father or mother more than me is not worthy of me: and he that loveth son or daughter more than me is not worthy of me. And he that taketh not his cross, and followeth after me, is not worthy of me. He that findeth his life shall lose it: and he that loseth his life *for my sake* shall find it" (Matthew 10:37–39). One perfect example of our Lord's declaration is that of missionaries Nate Saint, Jim Elliot, Ed McCully, Roger Youderian, and Peter Fleming—missionaries who were massacred by Auca Indians in South America years ago. Elizabeth Elliot and Rachel Saint went back to the same Indians and led many of them to Christ. That is total commitment to Christ—both for the men who willingly gave their lives for the cause of Christ and for the women who loved the Aucas enough to risk their own lives! And why would they do that? Because they took up the cross and followed the Lord.

You might say, "But they were missionaries. Missionaries often run into trouble." I guess you would be right. Apart from the Lord Jesus Christ, the Apostle Paul was the first missionary, and he certainly did run into trouble. But then you are also called to be a missionary, "For even hereunto were ye called: because Christ also suffered for us, leaving us an example, that ye should follow his steps" (1 Peter 2:21).

Christ is the example for everyone who commits his or her life to Him, everyone who is truly a child of God.

He suffered for you and me, and He expects no less from us. We are expected to follow in His steps. Remember the words of Jesus: "And he that taketh not his cross, and followeth after me, is not worthy of me."

Luke expressed the same truth that we saw in Matthew 10. But Luke takes a slightly different approach. In Luke 9:23–26, Jesus said, "If any man will come after me, let him deny himself, and take up his cross *daily,* and follow me. For whosoever will save his life shall lose it: but whosoever will lose his life *for my sake*, the same shall save it. For what is a man advantaged, if he gain the whole world, and lose himself, or be cast away? For whosoever shall be ashamed of me and of my words, of him shall the Son of man be ashamed, when he shall come in his own glory, and in his Father's, and of the holy angels."

Are You Acceptable?

To the praise of his grace, wherein he
hath made us accepted in the beloved.
In whom we have redemption through
his blood, the forgiveness of sins,
according to the riches of his grace.
[Ephesians 1:6–7]

The churches in America are often limited by people who seem to think that going to Heaven is dependent only on whether or not they claim to be Christians. Throughout my travels, I have asked a number of people whether or not they were Christians who responded in the affirmative, and yet they didn't know anything about Christ or the Bible. The plain truth is that if you call a donkey a horse it is still a donkey.

There is a doctrine that has been held for many decades dating back to the late nineteenth century, that may well have been a contributing factor to an apparent decline in the spirituality of many congregations. For lack of a better title, I call it the doctrine of "the acceptability of Christ." A. W. Tozer often referred to it as "a divided Christ." You have no doubt heard preachers give invitations on Christ's behalf by saying things like, "It's as simple as ABC. All you have to do is accept Christ as your Savior, and you are immediately saved!"

While I attended the Moody Graduate School, I sat under an instructor who had just written a small book titled: *Lordship Salvation, Is It Biblical?* In the book, he rejects everything I've said thus far. He rejects the need for repentance since repentance requires a turning away from sin. He complains that those who believe you must confess Christ as Lord deny the free gift of God and quotes part of what Paul told the Philippian jailer in Acts 16:31, "Believe on the Lord Jesus Christ and thou shalt be saved [omitting 'and thy house']. What he fails to say, however, is that one must believe on [again meaning commit oneself to] the *Lord* Jesus Christ. In the classroom this instructor said the word Lord simply means *Mister*, and all that one really needs to do is accept Christ as his or her Savior.

That makes a mockery of Almighty God. On the birthday of the Church, the day of Pentecost, Peter made this announcement: "Therefore let all the house of Israel know assuredly, that *God hath made that same Jesus*, whom ye have crucified, *both Lord and Christ*" (Acts 2:36).

Let me explain my understanding of what the Scriptures teach regarding the notion that we must find Christ acceptable in order to receive eternal life. Whoops! I'm sorry. The Scriptures teach *nothing* about this subject. I don't think the King of kings, Creator of the universe, and Author of our salvation is somehow impressed by whether or not we find His offer of salvation acceptable. The Lord of glory doesn't need to be grateful for our favor. The problem I see with the phrase "accepting Christ" is that it can't be defined apart from the definition I have assumed it to mean. Otherwise, what other meaning could it possibly have?

Oh, I know that some argue that it has just become a catchword for the decision to become a Christian, but that, of course, makes it a doctrine of salvation by works—a work of self-determination! It's like saying, "I have decided that I am going to Heaven." Such a condition, in itself, will cause many to assume they are going to Heaven, when the opposite may be true. One's relationship with God is determined by one's commitment to Christ as Lord.

Second, as I said earlier, there is no Scriptural reference for the term. As I study God's Word, I have an overriding rule that I follow faithfully. When it comes to spiritual matters, if it isn't in the Bible, it isn't true! The idea of simply "accepting Christ as your Savior" is *not* in the Bible! Some will say that it's just another way of saying "believe in the Lord Jesus Christ." That doesn't hold a drop of water because almost every use of the word "believe" in the New Testament means "to commit yourself to" or "to have faith in."

In John 2:23–24, we are given an account of those who were in Jerusalem to celebrate the passover feast. We are told that "many believed in his name, when they saw the miracles which he did. But Jesus did not *commit* himself unto them, because he knew all men." In this verse the word *commit* is the same Greek word that is most often translated *believe*. In those cases, the translation is "to have faith in." In other words, Jesus did not trust those Jews who outwardly believed in His name because of the miracles they had witnessed. It was a false "belief" on their part to the name of Christ, and Jesus would not commit Himself to them in any way.

How often I have heard a well-meaning believer tell someone that "all you need to do is accept Christ as your Savior," and then have that person repeat a prayer making that statement. Afterward, the would-be evangelist pronounces the person "saved." That "saved" person then goes merrily along in sin, never having either a personal relationship with Christ or a commitment to Him! Words alone don't save souls!

Only a heart-felt commitment to Christ as your Lord will do that. It's an act of confession, contrition, and repentance from sin. You'll notice that I did not include "works of righteousness." You can't be saved through baptism, tithing, church membership, or even "good behavior," because "we are all as an unclean thing, and all our righteousnesses are as filthy rags; and we all do fade as a leaf; and our iniquities, like the wind, have taken us away" (Isaiah 64:6)."

Nor can you be saved by declaring Christ to be acceptable to you! It's amazing that so many people believe in the "accept Christ" doctrine of salvation and label any other viewpoint as "salvation by works." Salvation comes by way of the gift of God's grace. We cannot save ourselves. If I were to say that I'm saved because *I* accepted *Christ* and not because Christ accepted me, that means that I saved myself. In other words, it places our salvation under our own control, our own authority, instead of God's authority. Our role is to believe what He has done for us and yield our lives to Him. What did God do to provide us with His grace? What gracious act did He perform? He sacrificed His only begotten Son on Calvary's cross! The shed blood of Jesus Christ was provided for us by way of God's grace! Then He raised Him from the dead. That's something that no one else could do. The grace of God is "not of yourselves: it is the gift of God" (Ephesians 2:8).

I have been reminded that since salvation is a gift from God, in order to receive that gift you have to accept it. Otherwise, it never really belongs to you. But that simply is not the case. When I was a child, Christmas was an exciting day for our family of ten. The children would leap from their beds and hurry to the Christmas tree and gaze in awe at the gifts. Each child usually had one or two presents lying under or near the tree, and we found it hard to wait to open them. At a given signal, we looked for the packages with each of our names on them. We didn't have to accept the gifts because they were already ours. After all, they had our names attached to them. Mom would say, "Those are Larry's gifts over there," and I would immediately grab them and tear the paper from the packages. I suppose one could say that Mom and Dad found me acceptable enough to give me the gifts of their own free will. The gifts were free indeed, and they belonged to me before I even knew where or what they were! When we confess Christ as our Lord with our heart by faith, the gift of eternal life automatically belongs to us! Our Lord purchased it for us and put our names on it!

Of course, Christ is never referred to in the Bible as a gift. That's an assumption based on an incorrect approach to "dividing the word." In John 3:16 eternal life is the gift as the result of Christ offering Himself as a sacrificial Lamb. He is, instead, the gift Giver.

Now there are only three verse references in the New Testament that refer to a free gift. Romans 5:15–17. These verses refer to the free *gift of righteousness* that is given to a believer. Verse 17 says, "For if by one man's offence death reigned by one; much more they which receive abundance of grace and of *the gift of righteousness* shall reign in life by one, Jesus Christ." In this case, two

67

gifts are referred to: the gift of the abundance of grace and the gift of righteousness. The Greek word translated "gift" in the Authorized version literally means *an endowment—something the Giver freely chooses to give.* An endowment is something that can be measured as in Ephesians 4:7, "But unto every one of us [every believer] is given grace according to the measure of the gift of Christ." In other words, Christ bestows a measure of grace to every believer as He chooses. That's why Paul called it the "abundance of grace." That's a measurable amount.

Ephesians 2: 8–9 presents another gift, a gift of spiritual protection: "For by grace are ye saved [*kept safe* or *protected*] through faith; and that not of yourselves, it is the gift of God: Not of works, lest any man should boast." In this case, there is a variation in the Greek. The word *gift* means *a sacrificial offering*—that is, the sacrifice Christ made of Himself. Our security is freely presented to us as the result of the shed blood of Christ. The safety or security of a born again believer, those of us who have been "quickened together" (Ephesians 2:5), is the subject. Jesus promised us, "I will never leave thee, nor forsake thee. So that we may boldly say, The Lord is my helper, and I will not fear what man shall do unto me" (Hebrews 13:5–6). Why? Because Ephesians 2:10 tells us that "we are his workmanship, created in Christ Jesus unto good works, which God hath before ordained that we should walk in them." We are re-created for a purpose beyond our salvation, and that is to fulfill an ordination to do good works.

Ephesians 3:1–2 tells us that Paul was given, or gifted, the dispensation [*administration*] of grace. In this case, grace is presented to Paul to pass along to the Gentile believers at Ephesus. "For this cause I Paul, the prisoner of Jesus Christ for you Gentiles, If ye have heard of the dispensation of the grace of God which is given me to you-ward . . . ." Paul was assigned the administration of the knowledge of God's grace to the Gentiles.

Finally, we are told that "the wages of sin is death; but the gift of God is *eternal life* through Jesus Christ our Lord" (Romans 6:23). Once again, the word gift refers to a *spiritual endowment*. Hence, God gives gifts freely to us—gifts of grace, righteousness, security, and eternal life.

Romans 5:21 states, "As sin hath reigned unto death, even so might *grace* reign through *righteousness* [*holiness*] unto eternal life by Jesus Christ our Lord." Isn't it interesting that the measure of the gift of grace that is meted out to us is based on the strength of our righteousness or holiness? Notice that Paul is talking about the two free gifts, grace and righteousness, as well as the gift of eternal life. This verse makes the difference between the effects sin has upon us and that of turning from sin to serve the Lord. A life in sin without repentance results in death—specifically the second death, the lake of fire—while living for Christ results in the rewards of eternal life.

We don't need to play word-games when it comes to the most important issue to any human soul. We don't need to create fanciful techniques or phrases in order to coax a lost soul to Christ. We need to tell it like it really is! Salvation is based on your commitment to and not your acceptance of the Giver. You are literally trading your life and soul for a new life in Christ. Christ, the Son of God, died an agonizing death on the cross. He paid a great price for the salvation He has offered to you. The price He paid was the purchase price for your commitment to Him. He gave you His life expecting you to give Him yours! You see, you are not accepting Christ, you are committing your life to Him for who He is and what He did to offer you eternal life. The plain and simple truth is that you cannot accept or possess Christ as your Savior without first confessing Him as your Lord. God said so! Every epistle in the New Testament is a guideline for following Christ in a life of obedience to Him. The Gospels are replete with instructions to follow Christ. In John 10:27–28 Jesus said, "My sheep hear my voice, and I know them, and they follow me: And I give unto them eternal life; and they shall never perish, neither shall any man pluck them out of my hand."

Ephesians 1:6 tells us that it is "to the praise of the glory of *his grace*, wherein *he* hath made *us* accepted in the beloved." In fact, it is not possible to come to Christ without being drawn to Him. Jesus said, "No man can come to me, except the Father which hath sent me draw him: and I will raise him up at the last day" (John 6:44). It is not the other way around. Our Lord does not want us to *accept* Him; He wants us to *commit* ourselves to Him. Colossians 3:23–24 exhorts us, "And whatsoever ye do, do it heartily, as to the Lord, and not unto men. Knowing that of the Lord ye shall receive the reward of the inheritance: for ye serve the Lord Christ."

Confessing Christ as your Lord is not based on your works. Your works are based on your commitment to Him as your Lord. Paul tells us in 2 Corinthians 5:17, "Therefore if any man be in Christ, he is a new creature;

old things have passed away; behold, all things are become new." Hence, if you are *in Christ*, you are a new creation, you are *His workmanship*, and you are created in Christ to *do good works* according to Ephesians 2:10. In fact, we are *ordained* by God to walk in those good works. It is to be our life-long activity. Why? Because the One who re-created us is our Lord, and we must obey Him. After all, that's why He re-created us.

By the way, there is nothing wrong with the word "obey." Romans 6:16 makes it clear: "Know ye not, that to whom ye yield yourselves servants to obey, his servants ye are to whom ye obey; whether of sin unto death, or of obedience unto righteousness?" We have a choice. We can obey the Lord Jesus Christ, thereby gaining eternal life, or we can remain in our old sinful state and perish in it.

"Aha!" some might say, "You do believe you are saved by works if you have to obey Him!" My dad's response would have been, "Hogwash!" The writer of Hebrews said, "Though he [Christ] were a Son, yet learned he obedience by the things which he suffered; And being made perfect, he became the author of eternal salvation unto all them that obey him" (Hebrews 5:8–9). I will readily admit that obedience to the Lord is not always comfortable, nor is it always devoid of work. After all, Philippians 2:7–8 describes the obedience of God's Son, the King of kings and Lord of lords, who "made himself of no reputation , and took upon him the form of a servant, and was made in the likeness of men: And being found in fashion as a man, he humbled himself, and became obedient unto death, even the death of the cross." Pity the man who would talk about obedience as though it were a crime for Almighty God to demand less of us or that somehow it would reflect poorly on his reputation.

A New and Living Way:

*Having therefore, brethren, boldness to enter
into the holiest by the blood of Jesus, By a new
and living way, which he hath consecrated for
us, through the vail, that is to say, his flesh;
And having a high priest over the house of God;
Let us draw near with a true heart in full assurance of faith, having our hearts sprinkled from
an evil conscience, and our bodies washed with
pure water.* **[Hebrews 10:19–22]**

We often misconstrue the phrase "not of works" in
Ephesians 2:9, thinking that it means that you don't have
to *do* anything to be saved. In other words, we can be
lazy to the nth degree and just sit back and say, "Here I
am, you lucky God. Take me, but please don't use me.
Don't expect me to do anything on your behalf."

In Acts 16:30, the Philippian jailor asked Paul, "What
must I *do* to be saved? Then Paul proceeded to tell him
what to *do*. "Believe on the Lord Jesus Christ, and thou
shalt be saved, and thy house" (31). Rarely do we hear
anyone explain what the phrase "believe on" means. Let
me repeat that the Greek that is translated "believe on"
is the word *pisteuo,* and it means "commit yourself to."
So if you believe on the Lord Jesus Christ, you are com
mitted to Him; and if you are not committed to Him, you
are not saved.

When we talk about confession, we usually assume
that we are to confess our sins to the Lord, and that is
certainly a part of confession. David prayed, "I acknowl-
edged my sin unto thee, and mine iniquity have I not hid.

I said, I will confess my transgressions unto the Lord; and thou forgavest the iniquity of my sin" (Psalm 32:5).

John said, "If we confess our sins, he is faithful and just to forgive us our sins, and to cleanse us from all unrighteousness" (1 John 1:9). When we confess our sins, God forgives us. We certainly can't forgive our own sins. Only God can do that! Then God cleanses us from all unrighteousness. Again, we can't cleanse ourselves. Only God can do that!

This type of confession requires not only acknowledging that we are sinners, but it requires repentance for the sin that has prevailed in our lives. I recently heard a nationally acclaimed radio preacher declare that "you don't have to repent to be saved; just accept Christ." This man, a former pastor of a very large church, has published Bible study books and CDs containing years of radio sermons, yet he seems oblivious to all the scriptures that exhort people to repent for salvation.

After His resurrection Jesus told His disciples in Luke 24:46–47, "Thus it is written, and thus it behoved Christ to suffer, and to rise from the dead the third day: And that repentance and remission of sins should be preached in his name among all nations, beginning at Jerusalem."

The word *repentance* is similar to the word *conversion*. "Repentance" means to turn our way of *thinking* around, while "conversion" means to turn our way of *living* around. Paul said in Philippians 2:5, "Let this *mind* be in you, which was also in Christ Jesus." That new mind-set can only take place when we have confessed our sins to the Lord and allowed Him to forgive us and cleanse the sins from our hearts.

Paul said in Colossians 3:10 that we have "put on the new man, which is *renewed in knowledge* after the image of him that created him." The word translated "renewed" means to *renovate* or *make new* or *clean up*. We are told that the new man has cleaned-up his way of thinking so it is like the One who created him. In other words, if you have repented and been converted, become a new man, then your thinking and way of living will be Christ-centered. That's what Paul meant when he said, "Let this mind be in you, which was also in Christ Jesus."

Peter told the Jews at Pentecost to "repent" for the "remission of sins." That's something you must *do* to be saved. He said in Acts 3:19, "Repent [turn your way of thinking around] ye therefore, and be converted [turn your way of living around], that your sins may be blotted out, when the times of refreshing shall come from the presence of the Lord." Notice that repentance had to precede conversion. If you don't repent of your sins, your sins will not be expunged, you will not be converted, and you will not be saved. On the other hand, if you have been converted, then you have changed your way of life from that of following after sin to that of following after Christ!

In Philippians 4:7–9, Paul tells us that "the peace of God, which passeth all understanding, shall keep your *hearts and minds* through Christ Jesus. Finally brethren, whatsoever things are true, whatsoever things are honest, whatsoever things are just, whatsoever things are pure, whatsoever things are lovely, whatsoever things are of good report; if there be any virtue, and if there be any praise, *think on these things*. Those things, which ye have both learned, and received, and heard, and seen in me, *do*: and the God of peace shall be with you."

Notice, Paul said that when you *do* the things he listed, then "the God of peace shall be with you." That means that if you don't do them, the God of peace will not be with you. While the peace of God keeps our hearts and minds through Christ Jesus, that peace—the peace that passes understanding—is not available if the God of peace is not with us!

Confession brings peace of mind, primarily because we know that when we have "made a clean breast of things" with the Lord, He has forgiven and washed away the things that have weighed us down with guilt and shame. David said in Psalm 34:18, "The Lord is nigh unto them that are of a broken heart; and saveth such as be of a contrite spirit." You'll notice that "the peace of God, which passeth all understanding" can only be ours when we have allowed the Lord Jesus to be the safe haven for our hearts and minds. The word translated "*keep*" in verse 7 means *to watch over* or *preserve.* That's what Christ does for us when we have confessed our sins to Him. That's what brings the peace of God to our hearts and minds—because we know beyond a doubt that we have found true forgiveness.

Having said all of these things, I do not mean to imply that a Christian will never again have to deal with sin. We still live in a body of flesh, and we will still be tempted by the things of the world. That's why Paul wrote in Colossians 3:1–3, "If ye then be risen with Christ, seek those things which are above, where Christ sitteth on the right hand of God. Set your affections on things above, not on things on the earth. For ye are dead [referring to our being dead to sin], and your life is hid with Christ in God."

We do have this reassurance in 1 Corinthians 10:13, "There hath no temptation taken you but such as is common to man: but God is faithful, who will not suffer you to be tempted above that ye are able; but will with the temptation also make a way to escape, that ye may be able to bear it."

However, when we have allowed ourselves to fall into temptation, we still have the knowledge delivered by John in 1 John 1:9, an admonition that was directed to Christian believers: "If we confess our sins, he is faithful and just to forgive us our sins, and to cleanse us from all unrighteousness."

Then Paul gives another purpose for confession when he said in Romans 10:9–10, "that if thou shalt confess [*acknowledge* or *agree fully*] with thy mouth Jesus as Lord, and shalt *believe in thine heart* that God has raised him from the dead, thou shalt be saved. For *with the heart* man believeth unto *righteousness*; and with the mouth confession is made unto salvation."

The verbal confession to other people that you believe with your heart that Jesus Christ is your Lord, proved to you by His resurrection, opens the door to the commitment you make. You see, His resurrection establishes the fact that He is the Lord of life itself, and when we acknowledge that fact to other people we also acknowledge that He is the Lord of our own lives!

That's why Paul added in verse 11, "For the scripture saith, Whosoever believeth on him shall not be ashamed." And that's why Jesus said in Matthew 10:32–33, "Whosoever therefore shall *confess me before men*, him will I confess also before my Father which is in heaven. But whosoever shall deny me before men, him will I also deny before my Father which is in heaven."

Knowing these things, you can understand why confessing Christ as our Lord is absolutely essential for our salvation. It has nothing to do with works, but rather it has everything to do with commitment. After all, why should Christ have committed Himself to us by the way of the cross if we are not willing to commit ourselves to Him by the same way.

As I said before, the idea of "accepting Christ as your Savior" is not in the Bible. In fact, just the opposite is true. *He* must find *you* acceptable to *Him*. Romans 12:1 and 2 exemplifies what God expects of us: "I beseech you therefore, brethren, by the mercies of God, that you present your bodies a living [Greek: *a life of*] sacrifice, holy, acceptable unto God, which is your reasonable service. And be not conformed to this world: but be ye transformed by the renewing of your mind, that ye may approve what is that good, and acceptable, and perfect, will of God." In other words, what God deems good and acceptable constitutes His perfect will. I often hear people ask, "How can I know the will of God?" Let's examine the subject since our Lord clearly wants you to know what His will is for you.

First, He tells us to present our bodies a living and holy sacrifice. In 1 Peter 3:15–18 we are told to "sanctify the Lord God in your hearts." That means we are be partakers of His holiness and His purity in order to consecrate our hearts to Him. Being sanctified by the presence of God in your heart is accomplished by your yielding to the Holy Spirit and enables you to "be ready always to give an answer to every man that asketh you a reason of the hope that is in you with meekness and fear. Having a good conscience; that, whereas they speak evil of you, as of evil doers, they may be ashamed that falsely accuse your good conversation [*behavior*] in Christ."

If you are truly a child of God, born of and sanctified by the Holy Spirit, then you must act like it. Romans 12:1 tells us that this is acceptable and reasonable. That means that anything else is neither acceptable nor reasonable. It stands to reason that if presenting our bodies holy and living sacrifices is acceptable to God, then if we fail to do so, it is *un*acceptable to God. If doing so is also our *reasonable* service, then our failure to do so is *un*reasonable.

We are to give our *lives* to the cause of Christ. Examine your own life. How much of your time, possessions, and energy do you spend for the Lord? How much do you suffer as a result of it? You might ask, "Does that mean that we have to suffer for Christ?" Paul tells us in Romans 8:16–18, "The Spirit himself beareth witness with our spirit, that we are the children of God: And if children, then heirs; heirs of God, and joint-heirs with Christ; *if so be that we suffer with him*, that we may be also glorified together. For I reckon that the sufferings of this present time are not worthy to be compared with the glory which shall be revealed in us."

Then we are instructed to "be not conformed to this world." John tells us in 1 John 2:15–17, "Love not the world, neither the things that are in the world. If any man love the world, the love of the Father is not in him. For all that is in the world, the lust of the flesh, and the lust of the eyes, and the pride of life, is not of the Father, but is of the world. And the world passeth away, and the lust thereof: but he that doeth *the will of God* abideth forever." Not conforming to this world, by renewing our minds [turning our way of thinking around] , and by living holy and sacrificial lives for the cause of Christ constitute the good and acceptable, and perfect will of God.

People often tend to read these verses from Romans 12 with what seems like a tongue-in-cheek attitude—especially those who stand in the pulpit and fail to fully explain the text which is more often than not the case. In the event one thinks that sitting on a hard pew and getting a crick in the back constitutes sacrificial living, he is from another world. Verse one states that if we are to receive the mercies of God, then we must present our bodies a living sacrifice. The Greek word for sacrifice literally means *to breathe hard* or *to smoke as by fire.* Even Webster's New World Dictionary gives two primary definitions. The predominant definition is the one exemplified in the Old Testament where animals are killed and burned on the altar (or the blood being sprinkled on the Mercy Seat); a physical sacrifice to honor God. It does not mean simply doing without something we want or think we need. The other definition given in the dictionary is that of a baseball play in which a player on base is "sacrificed over to another base." The fact is the player doing the sacrifice is put out. He loses his turn at bat.

What does this have to do with our bodies? It's quite simple. When we suffer, our bodies are the first to feel it, but it goes beyond pain. We can suffer without physical pain. We are told in 1 Peter 4:1–2, "Forasmuch then as Christ hath suffered for us in the flesh, arm yourselves likewise with the same mind: for he that hath suffered in the flesh hath ceased from sin; That he no longer should live the rest of his time in the flesh to the lusts of men, but to the will of God."

That's where the holiness aspect of Romans 12:1 comes in. "I beseech you therefore, brethren, by the mercies of God, that you present your bodies a living sacrifice, *holy*, acceptable unto God, which is your reasonable service." When we no longer allow the flesh to control us, to reign over our lives, our suffering begins. That's when we will suffer for Christ's sake!

Finally, Romans 12:2 establishes the very foundation of the new birth because you are "*transformed* by the renewing of your mind." That's called conversion, the result of repentance, and through this transformation His will is to deliver you from this present evil world according to Galatians 1:3–4, "Grace be to you and peace from God the Father, and from our Lord Jesus Christ, Who gave himself for our sins, that he might deliver us from this present evil world, *according to the will of God* and our Father."

I get concerned when I hear anyone say that "you don't have to give anything up to be saved. Just accept Christ as your Savior." That is not true! If you don't give up your sinful habits, you have not repented; you have not been converted. I've had people tell me, "I can't live the life. There are too many things I can't change." It seems like some would-be soul-winners are so concerned about winning others to Christ that they get desperate enough to try any ploy to make it as easy as possible, and they cave in to such feeble excuses for rejecting Christ. If you make it sound easy enough, then a lost person will readily say what you want him to say. That way you can boast that you saved another soul. It doesn't work that way!

I once sat under a pastor who preached about his security once he was saved and delighted in saying, "I am secure in my salvation. Now I can do anything I want to." That just isn't true! A Christian lives for Christ. If he just does what *he* wants to, then he is denying the Lordship of Christ. He must do what *the Lord* wants him to. That doesn't mean that he won't fail now and then, but his goal is to emulate Christ. We give up what *we* want to do with our lives the moment we confess Christ as our Lord.

Peter told the Jews at Pentecost, "Unto you first God, having raised up his Son Jesus, sent him to bless you, in turning away every one of you from his iniquities" (Acts 3:26). God gave this message to Solomon, "If my people, which are called by name, shall humble themselves, and pray, and seek my face, and turn from their wicked ways; then will I hear from heaven, and will forgive their sin" (2 Chronicles 7:14). God established His requirements for the forgiveness of sin.

In Hebrews 11:6 we are told, "But without faith it is impossible to please him [*God*]: for he that cometh to God must believe that he is, and that he is a rewarder of them that diligently seek him."

Paul said in Romans 6:22–23, "But now being made free from sin, and become servants to God, ye have your fruit unto holiness, and the end everlasting life. For the wages of sin is death; but the gift of God is eternal life through Jesus Christ our Lord." It's odd that some people love to quote 6:23, but never 6:22. Since we have become servants to God, His Lordship over us is established. There is no such thing as a servant without a Lord! Paul states emphatically that everlasting life is based on our being made free from sin and made servants of God. This is what gives us the ability to have "fruit unto holiness."

If one continues to allow sin to reign in his body, the wages of that sin is still death. A Christian has turned his life over to Christ so that Christ will reign in and over him. We can't have it both ways. Jesus said, "No servant can serve two masters: for either he will hate the one, and love the other; or else he will hold to the one, and despise the other. Ye cannot serve God and mammon" (Luke 16:13). In Mark 3:25, He said, "And if a house be divided against itself, that house cannot stand."

It was in *this* context that Jesus went on to say, "Verily I say unto you, All sins shall be forgiven unto the sons of men, and blasphemies wherewith soever they shall blaspheme. But he that shall blaspheme against the Holy Ghost hath never forgiveness, but is in danger of eternal damnation" (Mark 3:28–29).

Have you ever wondered what it means to "blaspheme against the Holy Ghost?" Think about it! It's that old "house divided against itself." It's having it both ways—trying to serve two masters—claiming to serve the Lord Jesus Christ and maintaining a servant relationship to sin! You will never be forgiven until you choose to allow Christ to reign over you because the wages of sin is death. You must choose which lord you will serve—Satan or Christ, the reign of sin or the reign of "fruit unto holiness."

I heard a preacher confess to one of his church members that he had launched into the man in a venomous tirade, then later apologized, stating that he had allowed Satan into his heart to control him. That's the old house divided against itself. His statement exposed the fact that this preacher was not a regenerate man, since the Spirit of God would not, and could not, share the inner man with Satan.

The preacher in question gradually began to tear down the church by treating other members the same way and chasing some away. He stole money from the church and became lavish with spending the church's money on things they couldn't afford. Then he began to pit members against each other. When the deacons confronted the preacher, his reaction was to declare that they couldn't do anything to him because he had only to answer to God. Only God had the authority to remove him from the church. That's where every cult begins! The next step would be for such a man to declare that he is equal with God and then very God. That's exactly what caused Lucifer's fall, and it's what caused the serpent to persuade Eve to seek the same power. Satan wields a heavy sword, and the church accepted the preacher's raving. They didn't realize that Christ wields a heavier sword—one that is "quick, and powerful, and sharper than any two-edged sword, piercing even to the dividing asunder of soul and spirit, and of the joints and marrow, and is a discerner of the thoughts and intents of the heart" (Hebrews 4:12). Christians don't have to bow to Satan's tyranny because "our God is a consuming fire" (Hebrews 12:29).

There were many complaints about the direction the church had taken, but no one had the spiritual courage or faith enough in God to take the necessary action of removing their "thorn in the flesh." As a result, they caved in to the enemy's onslaught and sought counsel regarding bankruptcy and church closure. They had been robbed of their spiritual backbone along with the financial means to pay their bills. That's what happens when the flock begins to disintegrate—to flee from the adversary rather than face him head-on. The would-be dragon slayers dropped their swords and retreated.

We have so much to contend with in this world. No matter which way we turn, we have three adversaries that are always there to cause us to stumble—the world, the flesh and the devil—and the temptations of today are greater than ever because the end of the age is approaching. But friend, we have something that nothing in this world can overcome. John tells us that "every spirit that confesseth not that Jesus Christ is come in the flesh is not of God: and this is that spirit of antichrist, whereof ye have heard that it should come; and even now already is it in the world. Ye are of God, little children, and have overcome them: because greater is he that is in you, than he that is in the world" (1 John 4:3–4). Notice that *the Holy Spirit is in you* if you are a born-again believer, but Satan is in the world and *not* in you.

For those of us who know the Lord, we know that we have a source of power that is greater than any other force in all the universe dwelling in us in the person of the Holy Spirit. Satan does not, and cannot, indwell us. Because of the indwelling presence of the Spirit of Christ, we can rejoice in the reminder in 1 John 15–17— "Whosoever shall confess that Jesus is the Son of God, God dwelleth in him, and he in God. And we have known and believed the love that God hath to us. God is love; and he that dwelleth in love dwelleth in God, and God in him. Herein is our love made perfect, that we may have boldness in the day of judgment: because as he is, so are we in this world."

85

So when we fret about the possible suffering we may go through for the cause of Christ, we must keep in mind what He did for us. "For it is better, if the will of God be so, that ye suffer for well doing, than for evil doing. For Christ also hath once suffered for sins, the just for the unjust, that he might bring us to God, being put to death in the flesh, but quickened by the Spirit" (1 Peter 3:17–18).

The writer of Hebrews reminds us of what Jesus did outside the gates of Jerusalem at Calvary: "Wherefore Jesus also, that he might sanctify the people with his own blood, suffered without the gate. Let us go forth therefore unto him without the camp [the way of the cross], bearing his reproach [your sins and mine that He carried to the cross]. For here have we no continuing city, but we seek one to come" (Hebrews 13:12–14).

Contrary to what many preachers are saying today, this present earth will be eradicated, and a new Earth will appear. The Jews look to the earthly Jerusalem, but Christians look for a New Jerusalem that will come down from Heaven to the New Earth.

You see, "in all these things we are more than conquerors through him that loved us. For I am persuaded, that neither death, nor life, nor angels, nor principalities, nor powers, nor things present, nor things to come, Nor height, nor depth, nor any other creature, shall be able to separate us from the love of God, which is in Christ Jesus our Lord" (Romans 8:37–39).

For clarification, let me repeat these basic truths: You cannot save yourself by works of righteousness, not by baptism, church membership, your generosity in giving, your moral standards, or any other action that requires your own initiative. If you choose to "accept Christ" as your Savior, that is a work of your own initiative! It is a declaration that you have selected His saving ability over all other religions, and it is purely an act based on your desire to go to Heaven instead of hell—motivated by total selfishness. In other words, it is tantamount to saying, "If you will assure me of eternal life, then I find that acceptable. If I'm not convinced that you will follow through, then I'll go somewhere else." The simple fact is, no matter how much you search, you will not find anywhere in the Bible where you are told that by accepting Christ as your Savior, you will indeed be saved.

On the other hand, by your relying entirely on the grace of God through His Son, the Lord Jesus Christ, by your faith, you will be saved! What's the difference? Well, under the "acceptance" notion, you are depending upon your personal intellect and your ability to decide whether or not Jesus is trustworthy. For your own convenience, you retain control of everything in your life. God has no say about anything! You have made no promise to give Him a place in your life. You have offered Him absolutely nothing. It's all take and no give, paying the Lord of all creation nothing more than lip service.

However, when you commit your life to Him, *He* assumes control of *your* life and your eternal destiny. As Paul said in 2 Timothy 1:12, "I know whom I have believed, and am persuaded that *he* is able to keep that which I have committed unto him against that day." If He is not the Lord of your life, He does not have the power, the authority, to guarantee your eternity. He has become just one more pawn in your quest to get everything you want for yourself.

Herein is the truth: when we commit our lives to Him, He retains His right to redeem what He has paid for—His purchased possession. If we don't make that commitment, there is no guarantee of our acceptance.

Everything I have said thus far points to the only authority that really matters—our Lord Jesus Christ. Everything that matters in life, we owe to Him. If it does not relate to Him, then it simply doesn't matter in life! Christians, and everything they possess, physically, intellectually, emotionally and spiritually, belong to Him. Our service and every breath we take belongs to Him. Those who reject that basic truth do not belong to Him. They have rejected or denied Him, and therefore, do not have the promise of eternal life because Jesus will deny them (2 Timothy 2:11–12).

Why is it that so many religious people reject some of the most important truths found in the Word of God? Nicodemus was one who recognized the truth when he came face to face with the One who was and is the way, the truth, and the life. He confessed Jesus as his Master and suggested that the entire Sanhedrin Council believed the same. They were the most powerful men among the religious leadership of the Jews, yet they had set up a system of doctrines and laws that went far beyond what the Scriptures even of their day contained. It has always been the case that human error creeps into many of our commonly held beliefs.

Nicodemus heard what Jesus had to say on that dark night and took Him at His word. He then defended our Lord before the Council in John 7:50, "Nicodemus saith unto them, (he that came to Jesus by night, being one of them,) Doth our law judge a man, before it hear him, and know what he doeth?" When Joseph of Arimathæa, a disciple of Jesus, came to take the body of our Lord from the cross, "there came also Nicodemus, which at first came to Jesus by night, and brought a mixture of myrrh and aloes, about an hundred pound weight. Then took they the body of Jesus, and wound it in linen clothes with the spices, as the manner of the Jews is to bury" (John 19:38–40).

Nicodemus called Jesus, "My Master." My prayer is that you are willing to call Jesus Christ, "My Master," too, confessing Him as the Lord of your life if you haven't already done so.

Examine Yourself:

*Examine yourselves, whether
ye be in the faith; prove your
own selves. Know ye not your
own selves, how that Jesus Christ
is in you, except ye be reprobates?*
[2 Corinthians 13:5]

We've covered a lot of ground in this section, but it
seems appropriate to recap the basic truths regarding
our relationship with the Lord Jesus Christ. We can't
have a relationship—we can't have true fellowship—
with Christ Jesus, unless we know who He is and what
He means to us. John speaks so passionately about our
fellowship with our Lord Jesus and with our brothers
and sisters in Christ. He makes it a standard for every
believer. He said, "That which we have seen and heard
declare we unto you, that ye also may have fellowship
with us: and truly our fellowship is with the Father, and
with his Son Jesus Christ. And these things write we unto
you, that your joy may be full" (1 John 1:3–4).

In order to have fellowship with other Christian believers, you must first have fellowship with the Author
of every Christian's salvation, the Lord Jesus Christ.
There are barriers to that kind of relationship. John said,
"that God is light, and in him is no darkness *at all*. If we
say we have fellowship wih him, and walk in darkness,
we lie, and do not the truth" (1 John 1:5–6). When you
walk in darkness, you have no opportunity for fellowship of any kind. There is a wall between you and God
that all men are prone, not just to build, but to maintain

in order to justify their own passions for the things of this world—things that fulfill the desires of the flesh. Of course, the one who is walking in darkness can't even distinguish what that means. His heart and mind are held captive to those things, and like a blind man, he stumbles through life.

As a graduate assistant at the university, one of my responsibilities was to tutor a blind undergraduate student. One experience with him will always stay in my mind. We were seated in his dormitory room as I read the textbook assignment to him, and the phone rang down the hall. The apartment contained several student bedrooms and a lounge.

Paul would have to answer the phone down the hall and around the corner in the lounge area. He insisted on his self-reliance and assured me that he could answer the phone himself. He hurried to his feet and down the hall. As he hurried down the hall I heard a loud thud and the slam of a door. When he returned, he was rubbing his head and said, "I told those guys to always shut their doors because I can't see when they are open!" He had rushed right into a door that another student had left open into the hallway.

I was not used to working with a blind person, and I learned something myself that day. I always checked to make sure his dorm-mates' doors were closed when I went to Paul's room.

You see, when a person is walking in darkness, he has many barriers to stumble into—barriers that stand between him and any potential fellowship with God—open doors designed by Satan to cause him to continually stumble. Those open doors represent temptations to keep him in the darkness of sin. In that darkness, a sinner will either walk through the open doorway to be swallowed up in more paths of darkness, or he will slam into the door and fall backward. Either way, his bondage is assured, and the tighter his bonds are, the more he blames the only Person who can save him from everything that goes wrong—the Lord Jesus Christ.

Anyone who is walking in darkness loves what he knows because he has never seen the Light of life. It seems like a contradiction. He loves his sin, but he hates the pain that results from it. Still he refuses to accept his own responsibility, choosing to accuse the Lord for failing to protect him.

You can't have true fellowship with a stranger. A person who is a stranger to God can only think of God as a stranger to himself. He will be bitter or angry because he doesn't know this stranger called Jesus Christ. He doesn't have access to the privileges that believers have, and when his prayers aren't answered (if, indeed, he prays), then he shakes his fist toward Heaven and curses the holy God whom he doesn't know anything about.

I know of a lady who has declared herself to be an atheist because, in her words, God doesn't answer her prayers. Seems to be a contradiction, doesn't it? She believes enough in God to ask for special favors from Him, but denies His existence because she can't communicate with Him! She is spiritually blind, caught up in the darkness of her own making. Instead of grasping for excuses, she needs to reach out to Jesus, confess her sins, and make Him the Lord of her life.

In order to have the kind of communication that she wants, she has to be in fellowship with Him, but as

John said, "If we say that we have fellowship with him, and walk in darkness, we lie, and do not the truth." It's strange that people want the benefits of God's fellowship but don't want the fellowship itself. How arrogant they are who think they have the right to God's undivided attention when they ignore Him or deny Him at all other times! They would tell us that God doesn't meet their demands when they fall into hard times or get themselves into trouble, but the rest of the time they want God to stay out of their lives and leave them alone. No matter how you peel it, they want to have everything their own way with or without God's help.

The Apostle Paul tells us that there are those who "walk in the vanity of their mind, Having the understanding darkened, being alienated from the life of God through the ignorance that is in them, because of the blindness of their heart" (Ephesians 4:17–18). These are people who choose to maintain their lives in sin and alienate themselves from the very One they want to make demands of. Paul describes the man who walks in the vanity of his mind in Galatians 6:3: "For if a man think himself to be something, when he is nothing, he deceiveth himself." They blindly grope in the darkness of their own making, then accuse God of failing them when things go wrong. How is it that such people can demand things from God while refusing to allow Him into their lives?

John went on to say in 1 John 1:7, "But if we walk in the light, as he is in the light, we have fellowship one with another, and the blood of Jesus Christ his Son cleanseth us from all sin." Aha! That's the proverbial "rub," wanting to "have our cake and eat it, too." But

Jesus made it clear that men love darkness rather than light because their deeds are evil. The only way to fellowship with Him is to confess the sins that have ruled their lives, repent, and confess Christ as the new Lord of their lives. They must know who He is and how He can give them everlasting life.

The first sermon that was preached on the birthday of the Church establishes the importance of the Lordship of Jesus Christ: Acts 2:32–36, "This Jesus hath God raised up, whereof we are all witnesses. Therefore being by the right hand of God *exalted*, and having received of the Father the promise of the Holy Ghost, he hath shed forth this, which ye now see and hear. For David is not ascended into the heavens: but he saith himself, *The Lord said unto my Lord*, Sit thou on my right hand, Until I make thy foes thy footstool. Therefore let all the house of Israel know assuredly, that God hath made that same Jesus, whom ye have crucified, both *Lord and Christ*."

In these verses we see that God the Father calls Jesus Christ *the Lord*! In verse 36 Peter calls Jesus both Lord and Christ [*the Anointed One*]. That may sound strange, but remember, God who created the entire universe by His spoken word tells us that a mystery "which from the beginning of the world hath been hid in God, who created all things by Jesus Christ: To the intent that now unto the principalities and powers in the heavenlies might be known by the church the manifold wisdom of God, According to the eternal purpose which he purposed in Christ Jesus *our Lord*." (Ephesians 3:9–11).

Notice that Almighty God the Father, by seating His Son on the throne at His right hand gave to His Son the authority to be *His* Lord. Then we are told that the intent or purpose in so doing was to make His Son *our* Lord! How could it be possible for Jesus Christ to be the Lord of lords and yet not be our Lord?

Now think about it. If God has yielded His Lordship to His Son, making Him the Lord of Lords, then it stands to reason that if we are to be called the children of God, we too must yield ourselves to the same Lordship. How can it be otherwise?

In Colossians 1:16–19, we read this amazing pronouncement: "For by him were all things created, that are in heaven, and that are in earth, visible and invisible, whether thrones, or dominions, or principalities, or powers: all things were created by him, and for him; And he is before all things, and by him all things consist. And he is the head [Lord] of the body, the church: who is the beginning, the firstborn from the dead; that in all things he might have the preeminence. For it pleased the Father that in him [Jesus] should all fulness dwell."

This passage tells us that Jesus Christ created everything, including you and me, by and for Himself, and that he is the Head [Lord] of the Church. Since He is the Head or Lord of the Church, He is the Lord over everyone who is a part of the Church. You cannot be in the body of Christ unless you worship Him as your Lord!

Romans 10:9–10 necessarily follows: "That if thou shalt *confess with thy mouth Jesus as Lord*, and shalt believe in thine heart that God hath raised him from the dead, thou shalt be saved. For with the heart man believeth unto righteousness; and with the mouth confession is made unto salvation." The Scripture declares emphatically that one must confess Christ as his or her Lord without hesitation—that is, with the mouth—in order to be

saved. Paul repeats this truth in verse 13: "For whosoever will call upon the name of *the Lord* shall be saved."
He doesn't say, the name of the Savior, but the name of
the Lord! Clearly, to deny this truth is to deny that the
Bible is the Word of God. It renders such a nay-sayer as
an unregenerate sinner. To reject Jesus Christ as Lord is
to refuse the salvation that He offers.

That's why the Lord Jesus said in Matthew 10:32–33,
"Whosoever therefore shall confess me before men, him
will I confess also before my Father which is in heaven.
But whosoever shall deny me before men, him will I also
deny before my Father which is in heaven." To confess
Jesus Christ before men means that you must confess
Him with your mouth: "That if thou shalt confess with
thy mouth Jesus as Lord . . . ."

Such a verbal confession shows that you are not
ashamed to be known as one who belongs to Jesus Christ
as your Lord. Hence, Christ warns, "For whosoever shall
be ashamed of me and of my words, of him shall the
Son of man be ashamed, when he shall come in his own
glory, and in his Father's, and of the holy angels" (Luke
9:26).

I wonder how anyone can debate or deny what God's
Word declares. In Philippians 2:9–11, we read, "Wherefore God also hath *highly exalted* him [Christ], and given
him *a name which is above every name*: That at the name
of Jesus *every* knee should bow, of [those] in heaven, and
[those] in earth, and [those] under the earth; And that
every tongue should *confess that Jesus Christ is Lord*,
to the glory of God the Father." Anyone who denies this
most basic truth of God's Word is guilty of calling Almighty God a liar! That is the very person that Christ

said He will deny before His Father and the angels in Heaven. That person will spend eternity in the Lake of Fire.

Every time the Lord Jesus Christ is so named, His name means three things. He is Lord (the *Supreme Authority and Master*), He is Jesus (*the Savior*), and He is Christ (*the Anointed One—the Messiah)*. His name tells us that He is *anointed* by the Father to be our *Lord* and *Savior*. All three designations are required to provide us with eternal life.

Consider these things. Lucifer rebelled against God when he fought to claim his superiority over the Son of God; Adam and Eve rebelled against God by rejecting the Lordship of Christ and attempting to declare themselves to be His equal; the Jews rebelled against the authority of their eternal King by having Him crucified, claiming to be superior to Him; and all mankind has rebelled against the authority of Christ, declaring their independence or freedom to live in sin—thereby making themselves slaves to sin and death and the enemies of Christ. The only way anyone can restore himself is to turn from his sinful rebellion and confess Christ as the Lord of his life. This is the *only* means of salvation recorded in the New Testament.

As a reminder, the work of merely accepting Jesus as one's Savior is *never* mentioned in the Bible. It is pure fiction! But it is fiction that can easily lead a person to think that because he has "accepted" Christ as his Savior he has the so-called "freedom" to continue in sin. There is no freedom in sin. Sin enslaves and condemns the sinner to hell.

There are those who argue that everything that smacks of works, or speaks of faith or righteousness, always refers to the work of Christ in us—that we have nothing what-soever to do with it. They say it is the Holy Spirit working through us. In other words, we *can't* do anything to serve the Lord. He does it all. Let me tell you that is sheer nonsense and makes God a liar!

Peter said in 1 Peter 1:21, in reference to faith and hope "that *your* faith and hope might be in God." Notice that he did not say that Christ's faith and hope in us might be in God.

James 2:17 tells us, "Even so faith, if it hath not works, is dead, being alone." Is it possible for Christ to have a dead faith? James goes on to say, "Yea, a man may say, thou hast faith, and I have works: shew me thy faith without works, and I will shew you *my* faith by *my* works." Did James take credit for what Jesus did for him? Certainly not. The Holy Spirit enables us to express our faith by our works, but that requires our willingness to obey Him.

Then in 4:17, James said, "Therefore to him that knoweth to do good, and doeth it not, to him it is sin." The implication according to the nay-sayers is that the failure of Christ to do good through a believer makes the believer a sinner! Now really! I am sure that Christ has never failed at anything.

Paul wrote to the Thessalonians, "We give thanks to God always for you all, making mention of you in our prayers; Remembering without ceasing *your work of faith*, and *labour of love*, and *patience of hope* in our Lord Jesus Christ, in the sight of God our Father" (1 Thessalonians 1:2–3). Once again we see Paul's recognition of the personal faith, love, and hope of those believers.

I could provide scores of references to the faith that is expressed by believers. The Greek word *pistis* translated "faith" means *persuasion. Pistis* is a derivative of the word *peitho* as in 2 Timothy 1:12 where Paul tells us, "I know whom I have believed, and am *persuaded* that he is able to keep that which I have committed unto him against that day." Faith or persuasion is not needed by our Lord, but is absolutely essential to the individual believer.

Ephesians 2:8–9 is a reminder to every born-again believer. When God says, "By grace are ye saved through faith," He is assuring us that we can accept His graciousness toward us as true—in this case, His graciousness in providing us with our salvation as the result of His gift [or *sacrificial offering* of Himself] because we believe Him when He says that He accomplished it on our behalf. Let me make it clear. The Greek does not say that our salvation is a gift as the result of our faith, but is, rather, the result of His sacrifice of Himself. *That* was *His* work, not ours. Therefore, no one can boast that the sacrifice was by his own effort. It was Christ's sacrifice of love and not ours. We don't have the bragging rights to any sacrificial work to obtain our salvation. The *sacrificing* was His work alone!

However, ask yourself: Is repentance a work of righteousness? Is confession a work of righteousness? Is commitment a work of righteousness? Is believing a work of righteousness? The answer to all of those questions is a resounding, "No!" No, because they are all required for salvation. It is by *His grace* through *our faith* that we are saved, but our faith includes all of these requirements. His grace is the gift of the sacrifice if His Son according to John 3:16.

From Darkness to Light

In him was life; and the life was the light of men. And the light shineth in darkness; and the darkness comprehended it not.

—John 1:4–5—

Out of the Darkness:

He brought them out of dark-
ness and the shadow of death,
and brake their bands in sunder.
[Psalm 107:14]

Proverbs 16:25 tells us, "There is a way that seemeth right unto a man, but the end thereof are the ways of death." And Proverbs 4:19 describes the way of such a man: "The way of the wicked is as darkness: they know not at what they stumble." There is a distinction made between the one who follows the way of the cross and the one described in the verses I've cited. Verse 18 of Proverbs 4 states that "the path of the just is as the shining light, that shineth more and more unto the perfect day."

When we hear sermons about Nicodemus, an issue is always made about the fact that he came to Jesus by night. We're usually told that the man was probably afraid to be seen with Christ for fear of what his fellow council members would do, and that may well be true. However, where Nicodemus was concerned, there was a far more reaching reason for his coming to Jesus under the cloak of darkness—a spiritual reason. He could have been numbered among the wicked men of Job's generation. Job said, "They are of those that rebel against the light; they know not the ways thereof, nor abide in the paths thereof" (Job 24:13).

Have you ever considered the fact that usually when men do things that are contrary to the will of God, they try their best to hide them from other people and from Almighty God, neither of which is possible? How many times have you read in the newspaper or seen on television that a famous person, whether movie star, politician, or athlete, has been exposed for some gross sin in his or her past? How many times have you heard a child say in front of someone else, "But Daddy (or Mommy) you said . . . ," or "You did it. Why can't I?" You've heard the expression: "Little pictures [or pitchers] have big ears."

Moses warned the people of Israel what would happen if they disobeyed the Lord: "But if you will not do so [obey the Lord], behold, ye have sinned against the Lord: and be sure your sin will find you out" (Numbers 32:23). Nothing is hidden from the Lord. You can do what you want in the dark or in the shadows, but the darkest room is like the light of the sun to God. There are no secrets. Those who would try to hide their sins from God are only fooling themselves.

Nicodemus was an important man in his society. He had everything a man of the world could want—wealth, position, power, and even an investment in religion. Still, this man was struggling with himself and questioning the very religious mandate that had been placed on his shoulders by those things that he valued so highly. He wasn't satisfied with his life, nor was he confident about his religion.

The fact is that he came to Jesus in the dark of night because walking in darkness was the only way he knew. It was his way of life. He struggled with himself and wondered why he had no peace. After all, he was still shackled to the curse of the law, and the law he was struggling with went far beyond the Levitical laws or even the Ten Commandments. The Pharisees had developed an intricate web of rules and regulations that can only be surpassed by our own government!

One might wonder how a man could be so thoroughly committed to the religious values that he grew from childhood to believe and still be so thoroughly dissatisfied and downright unhappy with them. How could a man like that gain such favor among his peers as to receive and possess such an important position of wealth, power, and zeal for his religion and yet spend sleepless nights in spiritual turmoil? Clearly, he couldn't sleep the night he came to Jesus! That was the dawning of a new day for him. He did the only thing he could do. He stepped into the light—the Light of Life.

Things haven't changed. There are many people today who think that success in life is tied to the very things that Nicodemus pursued. John Wesley preached for years before he realized that he really didn't know the Christ of whom he preached so fervently. One of today's most popular gospel songwriters and singers proved to be a spiritual disaster, and instead of turning to the One he wrote and sang so much about, he turned his back and walked away into a life of homosexual oblivion and total spiritual blindness. Through the years, there has been a parade of preachers, deacons, elders, Sunday School teachers, choir directors, and other church members who never missed a church service before they realized they really didn't know the Lord. These are folks who found Christ acceptable for so long for their own purposes but were never truly committed to Him. Over the years, the Lord has used our ministry to lead many such people to a saving knowledge of Christ.

The struggle between night and day, darkness and light, began in Genesis. You will recall that in the beginning the earth was nothing more than a thought in the

105

mind of God, nothing more than an empty space in the middle of an absolutely dark universe. There was no life of any kind and no life-giving light. It was only when God manifested His light that life could be created.

In earlier years, my wife and I lived on my parents' farm in Kentucky, and I remember so well lying awake at night listening to the constant shrill sounds of the tree frogs, cicadas, crickets, and an occasional scream from a screech owl. They were the only sounds of life. The cattle, horses, dogs, pigs, and chickens slept—unless, of course, some strange noise in the night caused the dogs to bark or the horses to neigh. The chickens could quickly be aroused when a fox or snake crept into the hen house—our barn. Even the morning glories that bloomed in the day folded their petals at night, awaiting the rising of the sun to bring them back to full bloom. The farm was surrounded by hills and trees, and unless there was a full moon, it was so dark that I could not have walked across the yard without the possibility of tripping over a fallen branch or stepping on a snake—both of which I have done.

One night a heavy fog had settled over our little valley and the narrow dirt road that led down the hill from the main road to our house. Dad had come home in the middle of the night from a job he held in town. His flashlight was useless in the fog, and he walked off the edge of the road into a deep ravine, tumbling over large rocks that had been thrown there to keep the road from washing away. He struggled up the embankment, suffering a number of bruises and scrapes, but fortunately, he was not seriously injured.

When we walk in darkness, it's much the same as walking in a fog. The road ahead will be dangerous, with many pitfalls and objects to stumble over. Our wounds are often much worse than those my dad had experienced—wounds that will have far more serious consequences.

Our Lord told the scribes and Pharisees who wanted to stone a woman caught in adultery, after challenging their judgment, "He that is without sin among you, let him first cast a stone at her" (John 8:7). He later told them, "I am the light of the world: he that followeth me shall not walk in darkness, but shall have the light of life" (8:12). In other words, they were walking in darkness as much as the woman. Without the Light of life to open their eyes, they didn't have the right to sit in judgment. It was a reminder of what Jesus had said at the foot of the mountain in Luke 6:41, "And why beholdest thou the mote that is in thy brother's eye, but perceivest not the beam that is in thine own eye?" The eye has nothing to see without the light.

The point is that, without Christ in our lives, we all stand guilty before a just and holy God. It is only through faith in Him that we can be relieved of that guilt. It's amazing to me how many people treat the sacrifice that Jesus made of Himself as if *He* were the one that owed the debt for *our* sin—as if the fact that He is the Lord of all creation is of no consequence! They behave as though they would be doing Him a favor if they became Christians. We can only begin our journey in the way of the cross when we realize that we are justified by the blood of the Lamb, the Lord of glory, which He shed freely on that cross. It was His favor, not ours!

107

In the eleventh chapter of John, we are told about the illness and subsequent death of Lazarus, the brother of Mary and Martha of Bethany. Upon hearing of His friend's death, Jesus told His disciples, "Let us go into Judea again" (John 11:7). But the disciples questioned *His* judgment. In verse 8, we read: "His disciples say unto him, Master, the Jews sought to stone thee; and goest thou thither again?" A good servant would have said, "Yes, Lord." How often have you responded to the still, small voice of God's Holy Spirit or to the Scriptures with "But, Lord" instead of "Yes, Lord"? How often have you questioned His judgment instead of following His leadership?

The disciples would learn soon enough. It was then that Jesus reminded them of what He had told the Jews: "Are there not twelve hours in the day? If any man walk in the day, he stumbleth not, because he seeth the light of this world. But if a man walk in the night, he stumbleth, because there is no light in him" (John 11:9–10).

When the disciples questioned the Lord's judgment, they didn't want to follow Him back to where the Jews had sought to stone Him. They had in essence rejected the Light of life and the admonition He had given the Jews earlier. It was His reminder about their walking in the night that brought them to their senses, and they chose to follow Him once again. As a result, they were able to witness the resurrection of their friend Lazarus.

Those who walk in darkness are always in danger of serious consequences—ultimately deadly ones. The Scripture warns us that, "The wages of sin is death" (Romans 6:23a). Ezekiel warned that "the soul that sinneth, it shall die" (Ezekiel 18:20).

I told about one of my wife's experiences in the Belgian Congo in my book *Christ in All His Glory.* It bears repeating here. As a result of that experience, Jeanette knows all too well what it means to choose between walking in darkness and walking in light.

During her teen years, she lived in the middle of the Kivu rain forest in the Belgian Congo with her missionary parents. Returning home one evening with her mother after a Bible study with the African schoolgirls, she began to shine her flashlight into the trees, paying no attention to what might lie in the path ahead. Her mother had warned her several times about keeping the light in front of them, but Jeanette was disobedient. She found out quickly what can happen when you step out of the light when her foot came down on the head of a black mamba, one of the deadliest snakes in the world of the cobra family. She had no choice but to stand still with her foot on the serpent's head. Had she removed her foot she would have been dead.

Jeanette's mother told her that she would have to go for help—but Jeanette would have to give her the flashlight so that she could see her way safely back. That was terrifying! There Jeanette stood for what seemed a lifetime in the darkness with a deadly mamba curling around her leg.

Her mother returned with her father who carried a *bupanga*, an African machete, to cut off the snake's head. How well Jeanette learned the meaning of what Jesus said in John 8:12, "I am the light of the world: he the followeth me shall not walk in darkness, but shall have the light of life."

The world is filled with snares for the one who walks in spiritual darkness, and the Apostle Paul warns us in Ephesians 5:6–8, "Let no man deceive you with vain words: for because of these things cometh the wrath of God upon the children of disobedience. Be not ye therefore partakers with them. For ye were sometimes [*in times past*] darkness, but now are ye light in the Lord: walk as children of light."

The Father of Lights has given you the golden opportunity to "let your light so shine before men, that they may see your good works, and glorify your Father which is in heaven" (Matthew 5:16).

The solution to the consequences of walking in darkness is found in Ephesians 5:14: "Wherefore he saith, Awake thou that sleepest, and arise from the dead, and Christ shall give thee light." That solution rests in your confession of faith in Christ as your Lord.

A Candle in the Night:

For Thou wilt light my candle:
the Lord my God will enlighten
my darkness. **[Psalm 18:28]**

What delights of life we miss when we reject the one true Light. Having the Lord of Glory in our lives makes all the difference, giving us a peace that passes understanding (Philippians 4:7) and enabling us to experience that "joy unspeakable and full of glory" (1 Peter 1:8) that is only found in the light of His presence.

He gives a light that will never fade away as though it were a candle in the night. It goes beyond this life into eternity. Peter tells us that we'll receive "an inheritance incorruptible, and undefiled, and that *fadeth not away*, reserved in heaven for you" (1 Peter 1:4). And John says, "God is light, and *in him is no darkness at all*" (1 John 1:5). In fact, 1 John 1:7 tells us that "if we *walk in the light*, as *he is in the light*, we have fellowship one with another, and the blood of Jesus Christ his Son cleanseth us from all sin." If we view these verses together, we see that our inheritance cannot fade away because it is ever present in perfect light, and as we walk in that perfect Light, we walk in Christ who *is* that perfect Light. Not only do we have fellowship with those in this life who know the Lord Jesus Christ because we share that Light, but we have an even closer fellowship with the Lord Jesus Himself, the Light of life. What more could we ask for?

What a difference we see in Nicodemus, a man who only knew what it was to walk in darkness. When Jesus told him about the new birth, Nicodemus responded with "How can these things be?" (John 3:9). His eyes were blind to the truth. Oh, yes, he had enough vision to recognize that Jesus was the Master and was sent from Heaven, but his eyes were blind to the one truth that would save his soul. In verses 10–12, Jesus said, "Art thou a master of Israel, and knowest not these things? Verily, verily, I say unto thee, we speak that we do know, and testify that we have seen; and ye receive not our witness. If I have told you earthly things, and ye believe not, how shall ye believe, if I tell you of heavenly things?"

The Lord was reminding Nicodemus that being under the Old Testament law, Nicodemus was in the process of breaking that law. The testimony of two or three witnesses was enough to establish the truth in any legal case, and there were certainly enough witnesses for Christ than the law required.

Nicodemus was blinded by his earthly knowledge— you know, the kind of knowledge that is foisted upon our young people by atheistic professors in our universities today. That kind of knowledge springs from pride, arrogance, and self-will and grows only in dark places like fungi in caves, where only bats and vermin exist. If we dare to let in a little light, they cringe and withdraw into darker corners—like roaches in a dark room when the light is suddenly turned on. Jesus told Nicodemus, "For every one that doeth evil hateth the light, neither cometh to the light, lest his deeds should be reproved [*discovered* or *uncovered*]" (John 3:20).

Always keep in mind that people live under the weight of sin. For the unbeliever, his propensity is to think and do things that spring from his sin nature. Hence, he will actively look for ways to undermine the gospel message and the truth of God's word while attempting to justify his own evil deeds.

Where believers are concerned, we have the defense that the Holy Spirit gives us, but it is still tainted by the flesh. On the one hand, we have the assurance found in 1 Corinthians 10:13: "There hath no temptation taken you but such as is common to man: but God is faithful, who will not suffer you to be tempted above that ye are able; but will with the temptation also make a way to escape, that ye may be able to bear it." As followers of Christ, when we are faced with what is common to man, we have the *uncommon* person of the Holy Spirit to provide protection from those temptations offered by the world.

On the other hand, we do still have what is *common* to the rest of humanity. We have a body of flesh that controls our behavior more often than we would like to admit. Those are the times when we must seek that spiritual protection. In other words, there is hope for those who struggle with this seeming contradiction in the Christian life because we have that which is *uncommon* to the rest of the world—the Word of God and the guidance of the indwelling Holy Spirit. They provide us with that way of escape. One can hardly ask God to bless him in whatever sinful behavior he is tempted to act upon. We have our faith in Christ and the ability to communicate directly with Almighty God. He *is* our way of escape! As Solomon said in Proverbs 3:5–6, "Trust in the Lord with all thine heart; and lean not unto thine own understanding. In all thy ways acknowledge him, and he shall direct thy paths."

No one can deny that in our weaker moments—moments when we close our minds to "the still small voice" of God—we allow the sin that is in our flesh to control our behavior. That's when Paul says, "It is no more I that do it, but sin that dwelleth in me" (Romans 7:20). That is also when we corrupt our relationship with God. "For to be carnally minded is death; but to be spiritually minded is life and peace" (8:6). To have peace with God, we must be spiritually minded. "For as many as are led by the Spirit, they are the sons [or children] of God" (8:14). Children are expected to obey their parents, both in this life and in the spiritual life. When we don't obey the Lord, then we are disciplined. Only until we have confessed our sin to Him will we have the sweet fellowship restored. In allowing the Holy Spirit to guide us, we are behaving as children should, and it is at that point that we can realize we are "delivered from the bondage of corruption into the glorious liberty of the children of God" (8:21).

Where Nicodemus was concerned, Jesus turned the light up to its full brilliance. Surely Jesus caught the man's attention when He said, "For God so loved the world, that he gave his only begotten Son, that whosoever believeth in him should not perish, but have everlasting life. For God sent not his Son into the world to condemn the world; but that the world through him might be saved. He that believeth on him is not condemned: but he that believeth not is condemned already, because he hath not believed in the name of the only begotten Son of God" (John 3:16–18).

When our wisdom and understanding is flawed by the world, the flesh, and the devil, it is difficult to grasp

114

the truth of God. Those evil influences warp our thinking, our logic, and the holiness of God's truth becomes illogical. How sad! But Jesus pressed on in verses 19–21: "And this is the condemnation, that light is come into the world, and men loved darkness rather than light, because their deeds were evil. For every one that doeth evil hateth the light, neither cometh to the light, lest his deeds should be reproved. But he that doeth truth cometh to the light, that his deeds may be made manifest [exposed by the light], that they are wrought in [*worked out by*] God." Anyone who is walking in the darkness of his own sin despises those of us who know the truth. They have no defense but to call us names, or tell lies about us, or to justify their own wicked behavior.

Now Nicodemus understood what Jesus meant when He said, "Except a man be born again, he cannot see the kingdom God" (John 3:3). After all, a man can't see where there is no light. Evidently, the light came on for Nicodemus because the next time we see his name he accompanies Joseph of Arimathaea to claim the body of the crucified Savior and to anoint it with a hundred pounds of expensive myrrh and aloes, to wrap it in linen and spices, and to lay it in a new sepulcher in a garden nearby.

Nicodemus wasn't the only person to receive the message of light. Jesus told His disciples in John 9:4–5, "I must work the works of him that sent me, while it is day: the night cometh, when no man can work. As long as I am in the world, I am the light of the world." But Jesus has ascended into Heaven and is seated at the right hand of the Father. Does that mean that we are all tossed back into darkness, or has He tipped His candle to others?

115

A Myriad of Candles:

That ye may be blameless and harm-
less, the sons of God, without rebuke,
in the midst of a crooked and perverse
nation, among whom ye shine as lights
in the world; Holding forth the word of
life. **[Philippians 2:15–16a]**

Jesus has placed in every believer an awareness of Himself through His Holy Spirit, who has taken up residence in our hearts. Paul tells us in 2 Corinthians 4:6, "For God, who commanded the light to shine out of darkness, hath *shined in our hearts*, to give the light of the knowledge of the glory of God in the face of Jesus Christ." In other words, He has placed His light in our hearts allowing us to reflect His glory.

A group of Greeks came to see Jesus in John 12. Jesus told them in verse 32, "And I, if I be lifted up from the earth, will draw all men unto me." The Greeks were confused by what He said, then he told them in verses 35–36, "Yet a little while is the light with you. Walk while ye have the light, lest darkness come upon you: for he that walketh in darkness knoweth not whither he goeth. While ye have the light, believe in the light, that ye may be *the children of light*."

The answer lies in that last phrase: "that ye may be the children of light." The disciples were not complete-ly aware of how the church would be established after Christ's ascension and that it would eventually become primarily a Gentile Church. After all, up to that time the Jews were God's only chosen people, but Isaiah fore-told what these Greeks were about to discover. About the

116

Gentiles, Isaiah said, "The people that walked in darkness have seen *a great light*: they that dwell in the land of the shadow of death, upon *them* hath the light shined" (Isaiah 9:2).

What, or Who, was that light that existed from before the creation? Verse 6 announces the coming of the Light of life: "For unto us a child is born, unto us a son is given: and the government shall be upon his shoulder: and his name shall be called Wonderful, Counselor, The mighty God, The everlasting Father, The Prince of Peace." These Greek (Gentile) visitors were to represent in type the coming Church—the children of light!

In Matthew 12:15–21, Jesus healed great multitudes of people and "charged them that they should not make him known: That it might be fulfilled which was spoken by Esaias [Isaiah] the prophet, saying, Behold my servant, whom I have chosen; my beloved, in whom my soul is well pleased: I will put my spirit upon him, and he shall shew judgment [*justice*] to *the Gentiles*. He shall not strive, nor cry; neither shall any man hear his voice in the streets. A bruised reed shall he not break, and smoking flax shall he not quench, till he send forth judgment unto victory. And *in his Name shall the Gentiles trust.*"

A remarkable account is given in the Gospel of Luke (Luke 2:25–35) of a man named Simeon, a man who had been anxiously awaiting "the consolation of Israel," the coming of the Messiah. The Holy Spirit had spoken to him, promising him that he would not die before he had seen the Messiah. Led by the Spirit, he went to the temple when Mary and Joseph were there to present Jesus according to the law. There he took the child "in his arms, and blessed God, and said, Lord, now lettest thou thy servant depart in peace, according to thy word: For

117

mine eyes have seen thy salvation, Which thou hast prepared before the face of all people; *A light to lighten the Gentiles*, and the glory of thy people Israel."

Isaiah 60:1–5 sheds more light on the subject in prophecy: "Arise, shine; for thy light is come, and the glory of the Lord is risen upon thee [Israel]. For, behold, the darkness shall cover the earth, and gross darkness the people: but the Lord shall arise upon thee, and his glory shall be seen upon thee. And *the Gentiles shall come to thy light*, and kings to the brightness of thy rising. Lift up thine eyes round about, and see: all they gather themselves together, they come to thee: thy sons shall come from far, and thy daughters shall be nursed at thy side. Then thou shalt see, and flow together, and thine heart shall fear [*shall be startled* or *stand in awe*], and be enlarged; because the abundance of the sea shall be converted unto thee, the forces of the Gentiles shall come unto thee."

Today's Church is comprised of people throughout the world, both Jews and Gentiles, who have confessed Christ as their Lord, receiving Him into their hearts and lives, and creating in all of us a light that outshines the stars—the Light of life.

In Isaiah 42:6, God speaks of the Messiah, the Lord Jesus Christ, saying, "I the Lord have called thee in righteousness, and will hold thine hand, and will keep thee, and give thee for a covenant of the people, for *a light of the Gentiles*." From Genesis through Revelation, God promised that multitudes from every nation, Jew and Gentile, would be redeemed.

When Abraham took his son up on Mount Moriah, which many believe to be Mount Calvary, to sacrifice him as God commanded, the Lord stopped him and provided a ram—a type of the Lord Jesus Christ—as a sacrifice instead. The Scripture tells us that "the angel of the Lord called unto Abraham out of heaven the second time, And said, By myself have I sworn, saith the Lord, for because thou hast done this thing, and hast not withheld thy son, *thine only son* [also a type of Jesus Christ]: That in blessing I will bless thee, and in multiplying I will multiply thy seed as the stars of the heaven, and as the sand which is upon the sea shore; and thy seed shall possess the gate of his enemies; And in thy seed shall all the nations of the earth be blessed; because thou hast obeyed my voice" (Genesis 22:15–18). This account opens the door of redemption to everyone on Earth—Jew and Gentile alike.

When God offered His only begotten Son on the cross, the promise to Abraham and the entire world of men was fulfilled. While Isaac was spared and a ram offered in his stead, "He that spared not his own Son, but delivered him up for us all, how shall he not with him also freely give us all things?" (Romans 8:32). For you see, Jesus was and is the Abrahamic ram or Lamb of God that was offered up once for all, sacrificing Himself on Calvary's cross and shedding His own blood so you and I could be redeemed.

> *Redeemed—how I love to proclaim it! Redeemed by*
> *the blood of the Lamb;*
> *Redeemed thro' His infinite Mercy, His child and*
> *forever I am.*

> — William J. Kirkptrick—
> "Redeemed"

119

The Children of Light
in a World of Darkness:

*While ye have light, believe in
the light, that ye might be the
children of light.* [John 12:36]

It may sound strange to compare the light that God revealed in this universe before He created life with those who are redeemed. There was no one to see the light, but when we realize that God provided the light of His glory in order to bring man into His glorious presence and provide him with eternal life up front, it makes more sense. Remember, *before* they chose to rebel, the Lord God told Adam and Eve they would live forever as long as they followed His instruction. Their rebellion caused them to lose the light of His glory. They stepped out of the Light of life into the darkness of sin and disgrace. Their sin was that of apostasy—the same sin that Lucifer committed when he rebelled against God. That's also when they realized their nakedness and tried to hide from the presence of their Creator.

Mankind is still trying to hide his nakedness from the Creator, still choosing to walk in darkness rather than stepping back into His holy light. Jesus told Nicodemus, "And this is the condemnation, that light is come into the world, and men loved darkness rather than light, because their deeds were evil" (John 3:19). Instead of receiving the Light of life and restoring that promise of eternal life, they choose to close their eyes and pretend God isn't really there. They dream up fantastic ideas in their attempt to hide from the truth, calling it science when it is no more than a pitiful attempt at denying the reality of God and His only begotten Son Jesus Christ. Paul wrote to Timothy, "O Timothy, keep that which is committed to thy trust, avoiding profane and vain babblings, and oppositions of science falsely so called [or *the knowledge which is falsely so called*]" (1 Timothy 6:20). They are like the proverbial ostrich who blinds itself by hiding its head in the sand, assuming that because it can't see anyone or anything else, then there simply must be nothing there.

Instead of recognizing the work of the Christ who created all things, men who think they have a greater knowledge than God try every trick they can find to make it appear as though God simply does not exist—as if they can close their eyes and make Him go away—and they go on with their efforts to prove their lies.

It reminds me of the time I spent the night at Grandma's house where I listened to Grandpa's ghost stories all evening. When I was in bed alone in a dark room, my imagination went wild. As the summer breeze moved the tree limbs back and forth, the full moon cast their shadows against the wall, and I threw the covers over my head thinking I could hide from whatever lurked in the room.

It's no coincidence that unbelievers today see the Father of lights as an evil presence, just as I had seen the evil shadows, when just the opposite is true. "In Him (Christ) there is no darkness at all" (1 John 1:5). Born-again Christians are being called all sorts of bad names and are listed by our military among terrorist organizations!

Now research scientists have announced they have discovered a part of the human stem cell that will enable them to double our life span within the next five to ten years. For example, as of this writing I am seventy-two years old. If I should live to be seventy-six or eighty-one, my life could be extended anywhere between 143 to 183 years. That will never happen. God has placed a limit on man's life span. If what scientists say is true, that means Jesus will return within the next five to ten years—or sooner—because God has appointed unto man once to die and after that the judgment! It's not the other way around. We all have an appointment with death, and that appointment was determined by Almighty God. God is the only one who can alter that appointment.

Such a concept, if effected, will usher in the coming of Christ and the beginning of the day of the Lord (or the day of God's wrath). The children of light are those who will escape "the day of the Lord"—that period of time that some theologians have labeled "the Tribulation"— the judgment that will be poured out upon mankind after the Church has been removed from the earth. But be- ing children of light requires a commitment on our part to serve the Lord Jesus Christ every day of our lives. Remember what Jesus said in Matthew 5:16: "Let your light so shine before men, that they may see your good works, and glorify your Father which is in heaven," and this we must be doing, but all the more so as we look for His return. In Luke 12:35–36, our Lord warns, "Let your loins be girded about [*be prepared* or *ready*] and your lights burning; And ye yourselves like unto men that wait for their Lord, when he will return from [or *for*] the wedding; that when he cometh and knocketh, they may open unto him immediately." In verse 40, Jesus adds, "Be ye therefore ready also: for the Son of man cometh at an hour when ye think not."

Religious people have developed a lethargic attitude about Christ's return and jeopardize their hope for eternal salvation—not having a personal relationship with the coming Bridegroom. These are the religious people 2 Peter 3:3–4 refers to: "Knowing this first, that there shall come in the last days scoffers, walking after their own lusts, And saying, Where is the promise of his coming? For since the fathers fell asleep, all things continue as they were from the beginning of creation." In verse 5, Peter tells us, "For this they willingly are ignorant!" Those are the ones who are not numbered among the children of light. The Lord will know His children by their burning and shining lights. 1 John 2:19 describes such people as those who are not truly His children, those "who went out from us, but they were not of us; for if they had been of us, they would have *continued* with us: but they went out that they might be made manifest, that none of them were of us" (NKJV).

Paul wrote to the Philippian believers: "Brethren, be followers together of me, and mark them which walk so as ye have us for an ensample. (For many walk, of whom I have told you often, and now tell you even weeping, that they are the enemies of the cross of Christ)" (Philippians 3:17–18. In other words, they are imitation believers "whose end is destruction, whose God is their belly, and whose glory is in their shame, who mind earthly things" (19).

To the children of light, Paul wrote, "For yourselves know perfectly that the day of the Lord so cometh as a thief in the night. For when they shall say, Peace and safety; then sudden destruction cometh upon them, as travail upon a woman with child; and they shall not escape. But ye, brethren, are not in darkness, that that day should overtake you as a thief. Ye are all *the children of light*, and the children of the day: we are not of the night, nor of darkness. Therefore let us not sleep, as do others; but let us *watch and be sober*. For they that sleep sleep in the night; and they that be drunken are drunken in the night. But let us, who are of the day, be sober, putting on the breastplate of faith and love; and for an helmet, the hope of salvation. For God hath not appointed us to wrath, but to obtain salvation by our Lord Jesus Christ, Who died for us, that, whether we wake or sleep, we should live together with him" (1 Thessalonians 5:2–10).

Paul opened his message with a reminder that Jesus is coming again. He is coming in the clouds to gather the saints to Himself—and that coming may be very, very soon. I believe with all my heart that the signs of the time point to his return in our lifetime—in fact, any day now.

Paul's exhortation tells us that when men least expect Christ's return, that's when He will come, and he reminds us that we who are the children of light must watch and be sober wearing the armor of faith, love, and the hope of salvation. Now let me ask you this: if you knew for certain that Jesus would come sometime between now and two months from now, what would you do to prepare for His coming?

I asked that question in a small Bible study group. One man shrugged and said, "Nothing." A woman said, "I guess I'd get busy and witness to as many people as I could." That answer exposed a lack of sincerity because, you see, Jesus *is* coming soon. We don't know the day or the hour, but we can readily see the signs of His coming building rapidly in our society and in our churches. If we truly believe He will return for His Church, perhaps in our lifetime, why would we not be actively engaged in His service at all times? Today's churches are filled with sluggards—imitation Christians! We have time for all the entertainment our small brains can soak up. We enjoy all the pleasures this world has to offer, and we think that if we sing in the choir once a week or attend Sunday School or simply fill a place in a pew, we have done our Lord a great favor. And most assuredly if we actually pray in a "prayer meeting" or even teach a class, we think we have reached the epitome of success in serving the Lord. Don't misunderstand, all of these activities are excellent ways of serving the Lord, but they are not the same as taking up the cross and following Him! The way of the cross requires a total commitment to Him and is the *only* way to be a true disciple of Jesus Christ.

Paul told us in Titus 2:11–13 exactly what to do when he said, "For the grace of God that bringeth salvation hath appeared to all men, Teaching us that, denying ungodliness and worldly lusts, we should live *soberly*, *righteously*, and *godly*, in this present world; Looking for that blessed hope, and the glorious appearing of the great God and our Saviour Jesus Christ."

How are you living right now? Does your life express the conditions that Paul sets before us? Let's look at what those conditions include:

First, in 1 Thessalonians 5 we are told as children of light (followers of Christ), as opposed to those of darkness (the lost), to *watch and be sober*. Those who are children of darkness by nature are spiritually dead—the ones who sleep. They are totally unconcerned about the coming of Christ because they have denied Him altogether. But those who know the Lord, the children of light, watch expectantly for Christ's return and pray without ceasing for His soon appearing. I pray daily the last prayer in the Bible found in Revelation 22:20. Jesus told John, "Surely I come quickly," to which John responded, "Even so, come, Lord Jesus."

I have emphasized the need for a sober attitude when it comes to our relationship with Jesus Christ. It isn't an original idea. It is found in 1 Thessalonians 5:6, "Therefore let us not sleep, as do others; but let us *watch and be sober* [literally: *to abstain from wine*] ," and in 1 Peter 4:7, "But the end of all things is at hand: *be ye therefore sober* [*be of sound mind*], *and watch* unto prayer." (Note that the first "sober" is not the same Greek word as the second.)

Paul told Titus to be "*looking for* that blessed hope, and the glorious appearing of the great God and our Saviour Jesus Christ (Titus 2:13), just as he told the Thessalonians to "*watch* and be sober." In Hebrews 9:28, the writer said, "So Christ was once offered to bear the sins of many; and unto them that *look for him* shall he appear the second time without sin unto salvation."

The implication is that those who are anxiously *looking* for or *watching* for His appearing are the true believers, while those who are religious but unconcerned about our Lord's return are simply nominal Christians. Paul specifies to "those who look for Him shall He appear the second time." It stands to reason that those who are not excited about His return are not His servants.

While we look forward with great anticipation to the coming of our Lord and celebrate the knowledge that we will finally reach our Heavenly home, our celebration must be tempered by the awe and reverence God expects of us.

Peter tells us to "watch unto *prayer*." Prayer is a trivial pursuit for most so-called Christians, and a typical prayer meeting in a local church consists of someone spending a half hour taking prayer requests and another half hour of members, seemingly welded to a pew, seeing how long they can wait for someone else to lead in prayer. They would never think of getting on their knees before a holy God in one accord. That's what happened at Pentecost, and who among them would want that kind of experience? Only exhibitionists would do that. Right?

But to the real believer, prayer is as essential to life as breathing. Lest that sounds extreme, Paul was an extremist *par excellence* when he said, "Pray without ceasing" (1 Thessalonians 5:17). Remember, he was writing to a church that thought they were already in the last days and looking for Christ's appearing. When kept in context, he specified several elements to our praying including, "Rejoice evermore. Pray without ceasing. In everything give thanks: for this is the will of God in Christ Jesus concerning you. Quench not the Spirit" (16–19).

If that all sounds extreme, you need to read the responsibilities that constitute the foundation for your prayers. He began with relationships with other people: "Now we exhort you, brethren, warn them that are unruly, comfort the feebleminded, support the weak, be patient toward all men. See that none render evil for evil unto any man; but ever follow that which is good, both

127

among yourselves, and to all men" (14–15). You might be thinking, *Paul must have meant somebody else. After all, we just don't do those things in our social venue.* Sorry. He was talking about the last days and looking forward to Christ's return.

Let's look at what he followed up with: "Despise not prophesyings. Prove [*test for approval*] all things; hold fast that which is good. Abstain from all appearance of evil [literally: *anything that may be viewed as evil*]. And the very God of peace sanctify you wholly; and I pray God your whole spirit and soul and body be preserved *blameless unto the coming of our Lord Jesus Christ*" (20–23).

Our Savior and Lord is gone from this world, and when He went away, He told us He would come again—come to take us home with Him. In the meantime, we are told to watch for Him and to pray—pray for those who are without Christ in their lives, and pray, "Even so, come, Lord Jesus!"

In Matthew 5:14–16, Jesus reassured us that the light of the world would remain after He ascended. He said, "*Ye* are the light of the world. A city that is set on a hill cannot be hid. Neither do men light a candle, and put it under a bushel, but on a candlestick; and it giveth light unto all that are in the house. Let *your* light so shine before men, that they may see your good works, and glorify your Father which is in heaven." We are the children of Light. His light must shine through us!

One might wonder how this could be. How could Jesus "transfer" His light to us? The answer rests in what Jesus told Nicodemus in John 3:5–8. He said, "Verily, verily, I say unto thee, except a man be born of water and of the Spirit, he cannot enter into the kingdom of God. That which is born of the flesh is flesh; and that which is born of the Spirit is spirit. Marvel not that I said unto thee, Ye must be born again. The wind bloweth where it listeth [*chooses*], and thou hearest the sound thereof, but canst not tell whence it cometh, and whither it goeth: so is every one that is born of the Spirit."

The Lord used the wind to portray the Holy Spirit because the Spirit of God applies the characteristics of the wind as He works in the lives of people. The Greek word for spirit is *pneuma* which literally means *a current of air* and applies to either a *breath* or a *breeze*.

Before we had air conditioners, we used fans to provide relief from the heat of a summer day. Many people still do. I remember so well the ladies of the church I attended when I was a youngster as they waved cardboard fans at their faces on those hot Sundays—fans that were usually provided by a local funeral home. In those days, folks didn't stay home from church on a hot day. After all, it was just as hot at home as it was at church. Of course, there were those who might have found comfort at the beach, but that wasn't my experience. The rare times I went to a beach I spent more time hopping around on the hot sand to keep from burning the soles of my feet! Even then I always came home with a blistering sunburn.

The point is that people use the wind to make themselves more comfortable, and we often see the word "Comforter" expressed in the Bible referring to the Holy Spirit. Jesus told His disciples in John 14:16–17, "And I will pray the Father, and he shall give you another Comforter, that he may abide with you for ever; The Spirit of truth; whom the world cannot receive, because it seeth him not, neither knoweth him: but ye know him; for he dwelleth with you, and shall be in you."

Notice that Jesus referred to Him as "another Comforter." Christ, Himself, was the Comforter who was present with them at that time. That's why He told them, "These things have I spoken unto you, being yet present with you. But the Comforter [Greek: *parakletos*], which is the Holy Ghost, whom the Father will send in my name, he shall teach you all things, and bring all things to your remembrance, whatsoever I have said unto you" (25–26).

The word *parakletos* is also translated as *intercessor, advocate,* or *consoler.* Hence, both Christ and the Holy Spirit are described as our Advocate with the Father as in 1 John 2:1, "And if any man sin, we have an advocate with the Father, Jesus Christ the righteous," or our Comforter as in John 15:26, "But when the Comforter is come, whom I will send unto you from the Father, even the Spirit of truth, which proceedeth from the Father, he shall testify of me." He intercedes on our behalf with the Father and provides comfort in our defense as we witness for Christ in this world. When we commit sin, Christ is our Advocate with the Father, and the Holy Spirit provides us with the consolation (comfort) we need to know that our sins have been forgiven.

The wind also scatters the seeds of the trees, the grasses, and the flowers that cover the fields. Even so the Holy Spirit, like the wind, wafts through the souls of those who confess Christ as their Lord. He scatters the seed of the gospel and plants it in the hearts of those who hear and believe.

Peter likens the souls of mankind to grass and flowers that are born of the seeds of the flesh in 1 Peter 1:24: "For all flesh is as grass, and all the glory of man as the flower of grass. The grass withereth, and the flower thereof falleth away." The seeds that are sown to the flesh will eventually perish—but not so of the seed of the gospel. Verse 25 continues, "But the word of the Lord endureth for ever. And this is the word which by the gospel is preached unto you." These two verses are clarified by the one preceding them. Verse 23 speaks of those who are "born again, not of corruptible seed, but of incorruptible, by the word of God, which liveth and abideth for ever." That incorruptible seed is sown by that Spiritual Wind that carries the seed of the gospel to the hearts of those who receive it.

The day is fast approaching when the Spirit of God will no longer sow the seed. You see, He requires born-again Christians to deliver the gospel that must be sown. But those who should be willing are no longer enthusiastic about carrying the message. That's why Jesus said, "The harvest truly is plenteous, but the labourers are few; Pray ye therefore the Lord of the harvest, that he will send forth labourers into his harvest" (Matthew 9:37–38).

In John 4:35–36, Jesus said, "Say not ye, There are yet four months, and then cometh harvest? behold, I say unto you, Lift up your eyes, and look on the fields; for they are white already to harvest. And he that reapeth receiveth wages, and gathereth fruit unto life eternal: that both he that soweth and he that reapeth may rejoice together."

It has been years since I've found a missions conference to attend in any church. Yet, in the years between

1940 and 1970, such conferences were a vital part of a local church's ministries. If you were to ask a church member today what missionaries his church supports, he wouldn't have the foggiest idea what you are talking about. My wife and I conducted revival and evangelistic meetings from coast to coast in hundreds of churches, camps, and schools, but today those same churches don't have the spiritual passion for souls they once had. Few churches today would even consider having such meetings. They are afraid they'll lose some of their tight-fisted dollars to send out men and women to win the lost to Christ or to bring in a God-appointed evangelist to do the job for them.

Everyone who comes into this world is born of water—the water of the womb. Jesus called this birth being "born of the flesh." However, to be born into the kingdom of God, one must be born of the Spirit, thereby gaining eternal life. That's why Jesus said, "That which is born of the flesh is flesh, and that which is born of the Spirit is spirit." But what takes place in us when we are born of the Spirit? Everything about us is changed, everything but the body we live in. Spiritually, we are new creatures!

A New Way of Thinking:

For who hath known the mind of the Lord,
that He may instruct him? But we have the
mind of Christ. **[1 Corinthians 2:16]**

The light of life becomes *our* light to the rest of the world through the indwelling presence of the Holy Spirit. We are assigned to the ministry that Christ presented to the world. In other words, we are to follow in His steps in presenting the Good News of salvation and present ourselves a living sacrifice, holy, not conformed to this world, but transformed by the renewing of our minds (Romans 12:1–2).

To be born again means to be made over into the likeness of Christ. The flesh takes a backseat, and the Holy Spirit takes the front seat. If one's behavior and mind-set hasn't changed, there is good reason to believe that person has not been born again.

Let me make it clear that we are saved by grace through faith and not by our works of righteousness according to Ephesians 2:8–9. However, we must also be aware of the fact that a change takes place when we place our souls in the hands of our Lord Jesus Christ. Jesus explained it to Nicodemus as being born again— born first by the water of the womb, the fleshly birth, and born again by the Spirit of God.

David declared that he was conceived as a sinner in Psalm 51:5, "Behold, I was shapen in iniquity; and in sin did my mother *conceive* me." That's what Jesus set forth as the process leading up to being born of water, or the fleshly birth. Every human being is born into this world through a mother's womb when that water breaks and the birth process begins. The sinful nature of that new-born baby, however, began at conception.

Contrary to popular opinion, an "age of accountability" is not found anywhere in the Bible. I heard Billy Graham declare that the Bible says that a child must make a decision for Christ when he reaches the age of accountability. He was wrong! There may well be an age at which a child becomes aware of his or her need for the Lord, but only God can know of such an age. My grandmother spoke often with me about my need to be saved beginning at a very early age, and frankly, I can't remember a time when I didn't believe in Jesus Christ as my Lord. I did make a commitment on two occasions: once when I was about seven years old and Grandma told me about the Rapture, after which I knelt in our backyard with my older brother and a youngster from my neighborhood, and we asked God to save us; and again when I was 18 years old during an invitation at a local church when the pastor challenged people to commit their lives to Christ. That commitment gave me a new outlook on life and my relationship with Christ.

At some point in every life, a decision must be made, a decision that will result in either eternal condemnation or eternal life. Everyone is eligible to pass from death to life based on that decision. We must either confess Christ as Lord or reject Him altogether. That's where the second birth comes in. When you confess Christ as your Lord and Savior you are born again, receiving a spiritual birth by being born of God. It's also when *conversion* takes place.

Now, I'm sure you've heard your favorite preacher say that "you don't have to give anything up to be saved. Just accept Christ as your Savior. That's all you have to do." In that case, you have been sadly misled. Salvation is the result of an act of commitment to Christ. The writer of Hebrews put it this way: "Though he were a Son, yet *learned he* [*Christ Jesus*] *obedience* by the things which he suffered [the way of the cross]; And being made perfect, he became the author of *eternal salvation* unto all them that *obey him*" (Hebrews 5:8–9]. Yes, God did indeed say that our eternal salvation is dependent upon our being obedient to Him. And how do we obey Him?

First we have to understand the meaning of the word "obey." In the Greek it means *to hear under* Him or *obey His command*. In other words, when He speaks, we place ourselves under the authority of His words.

A child begins his path to maturity by learning from his parents, and that learning is the result of obedience. My dad would always respond to my questioning his instructions—my asking "why"—with "because I said so." God expects us to follow the same learning process. We obey Him because He said so! After all, we typically reason things out from our carnal nature, and that nature is contrary to the nature of God. Hence, if we want to do what God wants us to do, we follow His instructions without questioning them. That's how we grow from spiritual infancy to full maturity, and that's what the rest of this chapter is about.

Paul warns us in Colossians 3:5–6, "Mortify [*put to death*] therefore your members which are upon the earth; fornication [*prostitution*, *adultery*, or *incest*], uncleanness [*impurity* or *demonic activity*], inordinate affection

135

[*passion or lust*], evil concupiscence [*longing for something that is forbidden*], and covetousness [*greediness, fraud*, or *extortion*], which is idolatry: For which things' sake the wrath of God cometh on the *children of disobedience*."

The specific commandments of Christ include those found in 1 John 3:22–24: "And whatsoever we ask, we receive of him, because we keep his commandments, and do those things that are pleasing in his sight. And this is his commandment, That we should believe [Greek: *have faith*] on the name of his Son Jesus Christ, and love one another, as he gave us commandment. And he that keepeth his commandments dwelleth in him, and he in him. And hereby we know that he abideth in us, by the Spirit which he hath given us."

The only way those commandments will work is if we are *converted*. Jesus said in Matthew 18:3, "Verily I say unto you, Except ye be *converted* [Greek*: turned around* or *turned another direction*], and become as little children, ye shall not enter into the kingdom of heaven." It's no coincidence that Jesus referred to *little* children rather than children in general. Little children haven't experienced the wickedness of older people. They are often referred to as *innocent* children (though they are not in fact totally innocent as the Psalmist pointed out). In other words, conversion requires that we turn to that condition that resembles a child's lack of interest in things of the flesh, things of this world, but one of reliance upon and obedience to its parents for guidance and nurturing.

Conversion takes place when we repent of sin and turn to a new life in Christ. Our old sinful man dies so that our new spiritual man can live. Paul poses the question in Romans 6:2, "How shall we, that are dead to sin, live any longer therein?" And in verse 6 he adds that "our old man is crucified with him [Christ], that the body of sin might be destroyed, that henceforth we should not serve sin."

How can we have a new way of thinking? A young woman in a church that we visited asked that question. "I can't think like Jesus," she continued. "He's God, and nobody can think like God!"

My answer is very simple and clear cut. By becoming *children of Light*! It's really that simple! Once we have made the commitment to follow Christ, we are given new minds. Philippians 2:5 instructs us to "Let this mind be in you, which was also in Christ Jesus." How did He think? What was in His mind?

I remember listening to a radio program many years ago sponsored by the *Radio Men's Bible Class*. Dr. M. R. DeHaan was the speaker. He was reading a letter from a listener who had asked a difficult question about the Bible. Dr. Dehaan paused, then gave a reply that was something like this: "God hasn't given me the light on this subject, but I will search the Scriptures, and when I have been enlightened I will share it with you." I am sure that he did just that on a later broadcast.

The point is that when we have become the children of Light, we have a new way of thinking and understanding. In 1 Corinthians 2:12–16 Paul tells us that "we have received, not the spirit of the world, but the spirit which is of God; that we might *know* the things that are freely given to us of God. Which things also we speak, not in the words which man's wisdom teacheth, but which the Holy Ghost teacheth; comparing spiritual things with spiritual. But the natural man receiveth not the things of the Spirit of God: for they are foolishness unto him: neither can he know them, because they are spiritually discerned. But he that is spiritual judgeth [*discerns, examines* or *determines*] all things, yet he himself is judged of no man. For who hath known the mind of the Lord, that He may instruct him? But *we have the mind of Christ*."

When we receive the Holy Spirit, a gift that is promised to every believer, we are no longer "the natural man." We have taken on a spiritual nature in the person of Christ by His Spirit. Hence, we have the mind of Christ. The only problem is that most believers don't know that, nor do they avail themselves of the fulness of His spiritual nature. We have immediate access to the mind of Christ, but we don't use the key to unlock the marvelous knowledge that He has made available to us through His Word.

Ephesians 5:6–8 explains what it takes to be a child of light: "Let no man deceive you with vain words: for because of these things cometh the wrath of God upon the children of disobedience. Be not ye therefore partakers with them. For ye were sometimes darkness, but now are ye light in the Lord: *walk as children of light*: (For the fruit of the Spirit is in all goodness and righteousness and truth:) Proving what is acceptable unto the Lord."

Then He instructs us to wake up and get dressed! "And that, knowing the time, that now it is high time to awake out of sleep: for now is our salvation nearer than when we believed. The night is far spent, the day is at hand: let us therefore cast off the works of darkness; and let us put on the armour of light" (Romans 13:11–12).

The Promise of the Father:

Wait for the promise of the Father, which, saith he, ye have heard of me. For John truly baptized with water; but ye shall be baptized with the Holy Ghost not many days hence. [Acts 1:4b–5]

This brings us to the very essence of the indwelling Holy Spirit. He instills in us the fruit of goodness and righteousness and truth—a purity that only He can give.

In John 3:25, we are told of confusion that had arisen among the disciples regarding John the baptizer: "Then there arose a question between some of John's disciples and the Jews about purifying." John called his baptism a baptism of "repentance" in Matthew 3:11. It was a ritual he used to give his followers a way to express their repentance publicly, and as a precursor to the baptism that Christ would offer.

However, their question afforded John the opportunity to explain the difference between the earthly form of baptism and the Heavenly form. His baptism could only cleanse the outer man, while Christ's baptism would cleanse the inner man. In Matthew, John went on to say, "I indeed baptize you with water unto repentance: but he that cometh after me is mightier than I, whose shoes I am not worthy to bear: he shall baptize you with the Holy Ghost, and with fire."

John's baptism was intended to *produce* repentance, while Christ's baptism is *the result of* repentance and confession. Believers today typically recognize baptism

139

as *a witness* to their confession of faith in Christ and their commitment to follow Him. It is not the same baptism that John performed. His was a temporary baptism awaiting the coming of the one true Baptizer—the one who baptizes with the Holy Spirit.

In Acts 1:4–5, Jesus met together with His apostles after the resurrection. On that occasion, He "commanded them that they should not depart from Jerusalem, but wait for the promise of the Father, which, saith He, ye have heard of me. For John truly baptized with water; but ye shall be baptized with the Holy Ghost not many days hence."

"Waiting" was not a part of the apostles' vocabulary. Their immediate response was, "Lord, wilt thou at this time restore again the kingdom to Israel?" (1:6). The problem they had was that they were used to thinking like the Jews. They could only see the kingdom as the historical land of promise, not realizing that the old kingdom was merely a figure or type of the coming eternal kingdom.

Jesus rebuked then in verses 7–8: "And he said unto them, It is not for you to know the times or the seasons, which the Father hath put in his own power. But ye shall receive power, after the Holy Ghost is come upon you: and ye shall be witnesses unto me both in Jerusalem, and in all Judæa, and in Samaria, and unto the uttermost part of the earth." His baptism, the baptism of the Holy Spirit, was to give them the power, or authority, to preach the gospel to a lost and dying world—*the way of the cross.*

Clearly neither John's baptism nor our testimonial baptism could ever change a soul. It saves no one and changes no one. Only the baptism of the Holy Spirit, the Spirit of Christ, can make such a change. Salvation comes by grace through faith. Faith includes *repentance* from sin and *confession* of Christ Jesus as your Lord and Savior, and Paul reminds us in Romans 10:17 that "faith cometh by hearing, and hearing by the word of God."

When Jesus came into Galilee, "preaching the gospel of the kingdom of God," He said, "The time is fulfilled, and the kingdom of God is at hand: *repent ye*, and believe the gospel" (Mark 1:14–15). Jesus told an "inumerable multitude" in Luke 13:3, "Except ye repent, ye shall all likewise perish." The disciples couldn't comprehend the idea that "the time" that was about to be fulfilled was that which led up to the cross of Christ. What lay between the crucifixion and "the kingdom of God" was to be the way of the cross laid out for every believer!

Paul said in Romans 10:8–10, "The word is nigh thee, even in thy mouth, and in thy heart: that is, *the word of faith*, which we preach; That if thou shalt *confess* with thy mouth Jesus as Lord, and shalt believe in thine heart that God hath raised him from the dead, thou shalt be saved. For with the heart man believeth unto righteousness; and with the mouth confession is made unto salvation." In verse 13, he added, "For whosoever shall call upon the name of the Lord shall be saved." Saving faith is based on the absolute belief that Jesus Christ was crucified, died, buried in a tomb, rose from the dead, and is your Lord. Once you have truly made such a commitment you have begun your journey in the way of the cross.

Anything that is added by anyone to the gospel that Paul preached is accursed according to Galatians 1:8–9: "But though we, or an angel from heaven, preach any other gospel unto you than that which we have preached unto you, let him be accursed [Greek meaning: *held in absolute and utter contempt* or *placed under a curse*]." To make sure his message is clear, Paul repeats his statement: "As we said before, so say I now again, If any man preach any other gospel unto you than that ye have received, let him be accursed." This means that anyone who preaches that baptism, communion, foot-washing, or any other ritual is required for salvation is accursed.

In John 3:27–31, John the baptizer answered the question asked by his followers in verse 25, "A man can receive nothing, except it be given him from heaven. Ye yourselves bear me witness, that I said, I am not the Christ, but that I am sent before him. He that hath the bride is the bridegroom: but the friend of the bridegroom, which standeth and heareth him, rejoiceth greatly because of the bridegroom's voice: this my joy therefore is fulfilled. He must increase, but I must decrease. He that cometh from above is above all: he that is of the earth is earthly, and speaketh of the earth: he that cometh from above is above all."

John tells his disciples that he is only an earthly herald of the coming of the Messiah. His baptism reflects the earthly nature of his approach. Basically he is saying, "I am not a heavenly being. Therefore, I can only illustrate in an earthly way what Christ can do for you on the spiritual level. My baptism must fade away, so that His baptism may flourish." Just as Jesus told Nicodemus that a man must be born first of water (the flesh or earthly birth) before he can be born again (by the Holy Spirit), John said that he could only baptize people with water as a means of expressing repentance, and only until the

Messiah came to baptize them into His body, the Church, the Bride of Christ.

To John's disciples, he could say, "I've shown you a picture of what you need to join the wedding party, and now, you can hear the voice of the Bridegroom Himself as He invites you in." Jesus is the Bridegroom, while John is merely a friend of the Bridegroom. He can get them to the church door, but only the Bridegroom can grant them entrance to the wedding. That's why John said his joy was fulfilled—completed. He said, "He [*Jesus*] must increase, but I must decrease." His earthly baptism must fade away, so that Christ's Heavenly baptism could become clear. John's disciples wanted to know what role his baptism played in the purification of anyone. John's response was that only the Holy Spirit provided by Christ's baptism could purify a soul.

In 1 Corinthians 12:13, Paul clarifies the relationship we have with Christ: "For by one *Spirit* are we all baptized into one body, whether we be Jews or Gentiles, whether we be bond or free; and have been all made to drink into one Spirit." Interestingly, it illustrates the difference between John's external washing by earthly water and Christ's internal washing by spiritual water. You can be cleaned up on the outside with water, but you can only be cleaned up (purified) on the inside with the well of water that springs up into everlasting life—the Holy Spirit (John 4:14). The only holy water is the Living Water of the Holy Spirit! John explains in John 4:2 that Jesus did not baptize anyone in water; however, His disciples continued with John's baptism until after the day of Pentecost. Then they gradually began to understand Christ's baptism—the baptism of the Holy Spirit which could not be accomplished until the Spirit was poured out at Pentecost.

This is corroborated by the vision that caused Peter to go to Caesarea to the household of the Gentile centurion, Cornelius, in Acts 10. Peter baptized those who received Christ with John's baptism (as exemplified in verse 37). Then as he recalled the event to the rest of the apostles and brethren, he said, "Then remembered I the word of the Lord, how that he said, John indeed baptized with water; but ye shall be baptized with the Holy Ghost. Forasmuch then as God gave them the like gift as he did unto us, who believed on the Lord Jesus Christ; what was I, that I could withstand God?" (Acts 11:16–17).

The Apostle Paul was keenly aware of this new baptism. In 1Corinthians 1:17–18, he said, "For *Christ sent me not to baptize*, but to preach the gospel: not with wisdom of words, lest the cross of Christ should be made of none effect. For the preaching of the cross is to them that perish foolishness; but unto us which are saved it is the power of God." Paul saw the difference between receiving the baptism of the Spirit of Christ through the preaching of the gospel and the earthly baptism of John.

This new experience had to be given to those who believed in such a very impressive manner so that they could fully realize what it meant for them to receive the most powerful force in the universe—the well of Living Water that was to empower and guide the church until the day of redemption!

That is precisely why Jesus told Nicodemus, "that which is born of the flesh is flesh, and that which is born of the Spirit is spirit." It is a simple task for a man to get wet on the surface, but it is a life-changing faith that enables him to be filled with the only Water that matters, the Holy Spirit. Remember, the Spirit of Christ is far more than empowerment for today—He is a well of water that springs up into everlasting life!

Man's hope has always been that he would never die. In books of fantasy, we read about people who are searching for the mystical and mysterious "fountain of youth" where anyone who drinks its water will be restored to his or her early years, or even to live forever. Sounds silly, doesn't it? But people today are searching for that elusive fountain by running to their medical doctors, physical therapists, reconstructive surgeons, hair restoration salons, among others, to regain or salvage their bodies to at least look younger than they really are. They try pills, diets, and various exercise programs that promise to make them look young again or add years to their lives. While it appears to be just a matter of vanity, if the truth were known, it's because nobody wants to die. They seem to think somehow that by changing their appearance or taking magic pills, they'll live longer. Even research scientists now claim that they can alter a person's genetic make-up that will enable that person to double his life-span. The truth is that we all must die!

Hebrews 9:27 tells us that "it is appointed unto men once to die, but after this the judgment." Some years ago we lived next door to an elderly woman who often made the comment, "Gittin' old is hell [her words]." She suffered a lot in her late years, both physically and emotionally. She told us that her son could hardly wait for her to die because she had a hefty IRA set aside as a part of his inheritance. At the time, we didn't know what was happening, but as her health grew worse, he began to withhold food and medicine from her. My wife and I had often taken meals to her, but the son ordered us to stay away. He didn't want us to feed her. "I'll take care of that myself," he told us. The lady didn't last much longer. That was why she felt that getting old was hell. I assume her son is the one who knows now what it's like to suffer the justice of God's judgment. He reminds me of the rich man who went to hell because of the way he treated Lazarus. Jesus said, "For what shall it profit a man, if he shall gain the whole world, and lose his own soul?" (Mark 8:36).

The only real hope that we can live forever rests in our faith in Jesus Christ as our Lord and Savior, and the only "fountain" that can accomplish that goal is the blood of Christ and the "well of water springing up into everlasting life." It is His Spirit-filled baptism that changes a man or woman from the fallen creature that he or she was to that of a new creature—a born again creation of God.

A New Way of Living:

As Christ was raised up from the dead by the glory of the Father, even so we also should walk in newness of life. **[Romans 6:4b]**

In 2 Corinthians 5:17 Paul tells us, "Therefore if any man be in Christ, he is a new creature: old things have passed away; behold, all things have become new." In other words, we have been born again; *we have become as little children.* That's what Jesus meant when he told Nicodemus, "Except a man be born again, he cannot see the kingdom of God" (John 3:3). But that means that our thinking and behaving have changed. Every sin we have ever committed has been forgiven, and we are given a new start in life just like a newborn baby whose thought processes haven't been manipulated and spoiled by sinful adults!

Jesus told the people in Jerusalem after He had been welcomed by the waving of palm branches in John 12:35–36, "Yet a little while ye have the light with you [speaking about Himself]. Walk while ye have the light, lest darkness come upon you: for he that walketh in darkness knoweth not whither he goeth. While ye have light, believe in the light, that ye may be the children of light."

On the day of Pentecost, God poured out His Spirit on those believers who were the first to experience the Light of life in a new way. The Holy Spirit is the Spirit of Christ who is now with those of us who believe in Him today so that we, too, can become the children of Light. We are given a new mind and a new outlook on

147

life. God's Word begins to unveil itself in new ways as we "study to shew ourselves approved unto God."

Philippians 2:7–8 says that "He *made of himself of no reputation* [Greek: *emptied himself*], and took upon him the form of *a servant*, and was made in the likeness of men: And being found in fashion as a man, he *humbled himself*, and *became obedient* unto death, even the death of the cross." Notice the progression of the nature of His mind. First, He set aside all concerns for himself— He emptied himself. That enabled Him to carry out His earthly ministry, suffer at the hands of other men, and accept His crucifixion. Remember how He prayed in the garden of Gethsemane: "O my Father, if this cup may not pass away from me, except I drink it, thy will be done" (Matthew 26:42). Our mind-set must be the same. Whatever lies in our path, our prayer must always be, "Thy will be done." People tend to pray for favors from God. Their prayers are much like blowing out all the candles on a birthday cake, thereby earning the right to have their wishes fulfilled, or like that old children's wishing star, you know, the first star one sees in the evening. The child recites a poem: "Star light, star bright, first star I see tonight, I wish I may, I wish I might have this wish I wish tonight." God doesn't rule the universe to grant wishes! Don't misunderstand, He does answer prayer but not just to please our fleshly desires.

There is a movement among those churches that fall into the Laodicean category that turns the favors or wishes into demands. They would *require* God to grant them their demands. "After all," they say, "we pay for it with our tithes and offerings." They call their sacrilegious philosophy "seed theology." There is little difference between the favors, wishes, and demands we send aloft. Seldom do we add, "Nevertheless, Thy will be done." Rarely, if ever, do we consider the admonition found in Hebrews 13:5, "Let your conversation [literally: *the way you turn*] be without covetousness; and be content with such things as ye have: for he hath said, I will never leave thee, nor forsake thee."

The Apostle Paul knew how to be content. He said in Philippians 4:11–13, "Not that I speak in respect of want: for I have learned, in whatsoever state I am, therewith to be content. I know both how to be abased, and I know how to abound: everywhere and in all things, I am instructed both to be full and to be hungry, both to abound and to suffer need. I can do all things through Christ which strengtheneth me."

Then we see in Philippians 2:7 that Jesus took upon himself "the form of a servant." Once again, we find that our purpose is to serve Him as our Lord—no matter where that service may lead. Jesus said, "If any man serve me, let him follow me; and where I am, there shall also my servant be: if any man serve me, him will my Father honour" (John 12:26). As one who has committed himself to Christ, you have become the servant of our Lord Jesus Christ and have vowed to follow Him wherever He may lead.

Hebrews 9:14 makes it clear that this is the reason for His sacrifice: "How much more shall the blood of Christ, who through the eternal Spirit offered himself without spot to God, purge your conscience from dead works to *serve the living God*?" One reason Christ shed His blood was to enable us to serve Him, but our service

149

has been perverted by a false perception of what service really means!

The Laodicean church in its state of apostasy has caused the churches of this generation to stray far from the goals that were set before us. We think that entertainment constitutes service. Wrong! Dead wrong! Because it involves dead works! I don't find any reference at all in the Scriptures to the entertainment service or a spiritual "gift of entertainment."

Church members are so spiritually lifeless that they would rather listen to raucous music and comedians telling funny stories than sit through an in-depth message from God's Word, especially if it exhorts us about commitment and evangelism. And oh the moans if we have to listen to an exposition of deeper doctrines. Mind you, I don't object to happy music or humorous anecdotes when used with good taste and with a purpose of applying it to the message from God's Word. My wife and I sing Christian music in our services, and I do use light humor occasionally in my preaching, but we always use such things to send a Scriptural message or to make a spiritual application.

My introduction to church as a new convert included a forty-five minute sermon in each service preached by a man who was serious about teaching and challenging the congregation, and when the service ended the people stayed for another half-hour enjoying each other.

I have had the privilege of sitting under the preaching and teaching ministries of such great men of the faith as the President of Wheaton College, V. Raymond Edman, Chaplain Evan Draper Welsh, Dr. Eugene Harrison of Wheaton College, Dr. Kenneth Kantzer of Wheaton

College, Sunday School teacher at Moody Church and editor-in-chief of *Christianity Today*, revivalist Vance Havner, Pastor J. Vernon McGee of the Church of the Open Door in Los Angeles and radio speaker, Dr. William Culbertson, president of Moody Bible Institute, MBI's G. Coleman Luck, Paul A. Evans, my late pastor and speaker for the Haven of Rest radio broadcast, and evangelist Billy Graham. I could list many more, and except for Billy Graham, as of this writing, these men are all with the Lord, and I'm afraid they would all be castigated for the length of their sermons and lectures in most churches today.

Today's church members major in the minors, avoiding at all costs any serious consideration of God's Holy Word. The brevity of the message outweighs the purpose of the message, and it takes no time at all to empty the building so folks can find something even more entertaining than the church social hour. The truth is that Hebrews 9:14 says that the reason for our salvation is that we are to *serve the living God* and not our hedonistic values!

Next we see that Jesus humbled himself. The Greek word translated "humbled" means to *depress* or *humiliate* ones self. The King of kings was completely humiliated when He was tried in a kangaroo court, slapped in the face, spat upon, crowned with thorns, stripped naked, and nailed to a cross!

In 2 Corinthians 11:24–27, the Apostle Paul expressed his own humiliation this way: "Of the Jews five times received I forty stripes save one. Thrice was I beaten with rods, once I was stoned, thrice I suffered shipwreck, a night and a day I have been in the deep; In journeyings often, in perils of waters, in perils of robbers, in perils of mine own countrymen, in perils by the heathen, in perils in the city, in perils in the wilderness, in perils in the sea, in perils among false brethren, In weariness and painfulness, in watchings often, in hunger and thirst, in fastings often, in cold and nakedness."

In spite of all his sufferings, Paul wrote to Timothy from prison, "I am now ready to be offered, and the time of my departure is at hand. I have fought a good fight, I have finished my course, I have kept the faith: Henceforth there is laid up for me a crown of righteousness, which the Lord, the righteous judge, shall give me at that day: and not to me only, but unto all them also that love his appearing" (2 Timothy 4:6–8).

Think about it. Will you receive a crown of righteousness when Christ returns to call His Church away? If so, why? Why should you? Do you love His promised appearing when He does return? You might be surprised to know that among the hundreds of churches where the Rudder family has conducted meetings, I have had scores of church members tell me that they aren't looking forward to His return. They express several reasons such as, "I am not ready," or "There are things I need to do," or "I have loved ones who need to be saved." None of those reasons are worth their salt because they have absolutely no bearing on His return for His Church, and I am quick to tell them that Christ will come only for those who look eagerly for His coming.

Colossians 3:1–4 sounds a note of both exhortation and rejoicing: "If ye then be risen with Christ, seek those things which are above, where Christ sitteth on the right hand of God. Set your affections on things above, not on things on the earth. For ye are dead, and your life is hid with Christ in God. When Christ who is our life, shall appear, then shall ye also appear with him in glory."

It doesn't take much consideration to compare the brevity of the present with our eternal abode. The Psalmist reminds us that "Man is like to vanity: his days are as a shadow that passeth away" (Psalm 144:4). In Psalm 102:11–12, he said, "My days are like a shadow that declineth; and I am withered like grass. But thou, O Lord, shalt endure for ever." There is no comparison between the here and now and eternity! That's one reason the gathering of the saints to meet the Lord in the air must be an exciting time, an event that causes us to rejoice, and a Christian who is concerned about his readiness is not living an obedient spiritual life.

One older lady who had just found out that she was suffering with a serious illness told me that she didn't want to die. I told her that death was not something to be feared for those who know the Lord. Hebrews 9:26–28 declares that "now once in the end of the world hath he appeared to put away sin by the sacrifice of himself. And as *it is appointed unto men once to die*, but after this the judgment: So Christ was once offered to bear the sins of many; and unto them that *look for him* shall he appear the second time without sin unto salvation."

According to God's Word you have an appointment with death. Not only so, but if you are a born-again Christian, you also have a scheduled court appearance at the judgment seat of Christ. If you are not a Christian, you must appear at the great white throne judgment.

The lady's problem was that she wasn't where she should have been spiritually, so she was unwilling to face the judge. I speak about her in the past tense because she is now in His hands. When you are not living an obedient life, you will most certainly not be enthusiastic about our Lord's glorious appearing in the clouds!

Paul wrote to Titus, "For the grace of God that bringeth salvation hath appeared to all men, Teaching us that, denying ungodliness and worldly lusts, we should live soberly, righteously, and godly, in this present world; Looking for that blessed hope, and the glorious appearing of the great God and our Saviour Jesus Christ; Who gave himself for us, that he might redeem us from all iniquity, and purify unto himself a peculiar people, zealous of good works." (Titus 2:11–14)

The lady in question, though claiming to be a Christian, was not living a godly life. How can anyone look forward to meeting Jesus face-to-face if he or she is not meeting the minimum standards of conduct that He has assigned to us? We are to deny ungodliness and worldly lusts. I realize that isn't a popular position to hold in today's churches, but to "live soberly, righteously, and godly, in this present world" is not an easy thing to do, especially when you are being pulled in the opposite direction, and especially when there are hypocrites in the pulpits declaring "Because I am saved by grace, I can do anything I want to do. I just don't want to." Yes, I have heard more than one preacher make that declaration. The one who stands out the most in my mind was the pastor of a church that I once attended. The man walked into a meeting at the church and announced, "I am no longer fit to be a minister," then turned and walked out. He evidently had a brief change of mind about whether or not he wanted to! In such a case, he wouldn't be "looking for that blessed hope, and the glorious appearing of the great God and our Saviour Jesus Christ," either, especially with the knowledge that He "gave himself for us, that He might redeem us from all iniquity, and purify unto himself a peculiar people, zealous of good works."

Perhaps the word *purify* scares us. Our Lord died to redeem people from iniquity and purify them to the extent that they would be seen as "peculiar." No one wants to be seen as different or peculiar, but the fact is that if you are not, then you are not meeting the requirements of the Christian faith as God has spelled it out for us. Look at Hebrews 12:14–15a: "Follow peace with all men, and *holiness, without which no man shall see the Lord: Looking diligently* lest any man fail of the grace of God."

The Greek word translated "holiness" means "moral purity" or "sanctification." This verse states flatly that without moral purity no man shall see the Lord. According to the Word of God, what man shall see the Lord without holiness? Honesty requires only one answer: None!

The expression "lest any man fail [*fall short*] of the grace of God" is comparable to Romans 3:23, "For all have sinned and come short of the glory of God." The expression "come short" is the same one translated "fail" in Hebrews 12:15. Falling short of the grace of God means that one hasn't reached the point of experiencing God's grace, and it's by God's grace that we are saved. Hence, according to Hebrews 12:14, we are warned to beware because without holiness, we cannot see the Lord. Verse 15 tells us it's because we have fallen short of God's grace.

I have always made it clear that one cannot arrive at a doctrinal conclusion solely on the basis of one verse of Scripture. So it is appropriate to re-examine John's statement in 1 John 3:2–3: "Beloved, now are we the sons of God, and it doth not yet appear what we shall be: but we know that, when he shall appear, we shall be like him; for we shall see him as he is. And every man that hath this hope [the hope of glory] in him *purifieth himself, even as he is pure.*" John said that our hope of glory is tied to our moral purity. But remember that this entire concept is based on the fact that a change takes place in our hearts and minds when we confess Christ as our Lord—a change called "conversion."

We cannot be saved by works. Salvation is by grace through faith. However, when the Holy Spirit enters our temple, we are dramatically changed. Let me refresh your memory since we have traveled so far on this subject. 2 Corinthians 5:17 tells us, "Therefore if any man be in Christ, he is a new creature: old things have passed away; behold, all things have become new." He has been born again by the Holy Spirit; he has been converted. At that moment he is made righteous, holy, purified. His sins have been cleansed or washed away by the blood of the Lamb. Now he is a new creature committed to obeying the Lord Jesus Christ.

That doesn't mean that a born-again Christian will never fail the Lord, but it does mean that moral purity can be regained when we confess our sins. John gives us that assurance in 1 John 1:9, "If we confess our sins, he is faithful and just to forgive us our sins, and to cleanse us from all unrighteousness."

156

Remember, too, that we are talking about the reasons people give for not looking forward to the day of redemption, what most people call "the Rapture," when Jesus comes to call His Church away. These are people who will not be looking for His coming.

To the one who says he is not ready, then my response is that he never will be ready—at least not until he has confessed Christ as his Lord and Savior. If he is not ready, then he is not born again! If he says that there are things he needs or wants to accomplish before the Lord calls him away, then what he thinks he needs to do is simply not important—not important enough to miss the opportunity to be saved. Otherwise, he would already have done the things that he thinks he needs to accomplish.

The fact is that if anything is more important to anyone than his eternal salvation and the needs of others, then once again, he is not born again. The truly regenerate believer is anxiously awaiting our Lord's return! And if a man says that he has loved ones who still need to be saved, then I must ask him, "Why? What have you been doing all this time that is more important than your making serious efforts at bringing them to a saving knowledge of Christ?" Now if he has made every effort at doing so, and they are still not saved, then the eternal well-being of those who have rejected Jesus as Lord is in their own hands.

You see, like it or not, not everyone is going to be saved. There is a vast and still growing world of people who will never come to Christ, and even fewer to be saved because the Church is crumbling into apostasy and failing to obey the Lord. The issue each one must reckon with is whether or not he or she *chooses* to confess Christ as Lord or chooses to deny Him. The choice is always left up to us. No one can be coerced into receiving Jesus Christ into his life. That may sound harsh, but it is the way God determined it to be. That same choice was given to Adam and Eve, and they chose to deny Him bringing death upon themselves and the rest of God's creation.

The difference today is that Christ died for our sins and provided us with the choice to be redeemed or not. As Joshua said to the people of Israel in Joshua 24:15, "Choose you this day whom ye will serve . . . but as for me and my house, we will serve the Lord."

However, there is another point of view regarding the one who has exhausted his attempts at leading a loved one to Christ. Has he met the standards required by our Lord necessary to be a witness of His saving grace? One cannot convince another person of his need for salvation if he hasn't manifested the characteristics of a born-again Christian.

That brings up another general fear for the coming of Christ: "But there are still too many people who need to be saved throughout the world!" Of course there are! And, as I said, every day that passes there will be many, many more born into the world who will never be saved! The argument falls flat on its face. While we sit in our pews enjoying entertaining church services, millions will perish and spend eternity in hell! And in this age of apostasy it will only get worse. That is the fault of the fallen churches and every believer who fails to serve the Lord. Little wonder that so many envision the coming of Christ with fear and trembling.

But you must remember that every living soul is ultimately responsible for his own decision to confess or deny the authority of Christ in his life. Authority is what mankind rebels against, and certainly the one who rejects Christ is a rebel who will not yield himself to the lordship of Jesus Christ. Anyone who is truly converted has placed himself under the leadership and control of the Son of God.

It is no coincidence that John wrote in 1 John 2:1–4, "My little children, these things write I unto you, that ye sin not. And if any man sin, we have an advocate with the Father, Jesus Christ the righteous: And he is the propitiation for our sins; and not for ours only, but also for the sins of the whole world. And hereby we do know that we know him, if we keep his commandments. He that saith, I know him, and keepeth not his commandments, is a liar, and the truth is not in him."

This brings us back to the two commandments I mentioned earlier. The commandments John referred to are the two great commandments described in a precise way in 1 John 3:23: "And this is his commandment, That we should believe on the name of his Son Jesus Christ, and love one another, as he gave us commandment." What he literally said was that if you don't believe in the Son of God, you don't love the Lord your God, and if you don't love one another, you don't love your ncighbor [Grcck: *near one*].

But he also said that if you don't keep these commandments, you are a liar, and the truth is not in you. Don't forget that Jesus Christ *is* the truth. That's why he added in verse 24: "And he that keepeth his commandments dwelleth in Him, and He in him. And hereby we

159

know that he abideth in us, by the Spirit which he hath given us."

The first commandment explains the meaning of Revelation 21:8 where we are told that among other sins, "*all* liars shall have their part in the lake which burneth with fire and brimstone: which is the second death." You might be confused knowing that everyone has lied at one time or another. Does that mean that everyone will be cast into the lake of fire? John answers the question in 1 John 2:22–23: "Who is a liar but he that denieth that Jesus is the Christ? He is antichrist, that denieth the father and the Son. Whosoever denieth the Son, the same hath not the Father: he that acknowledgeth the Son hath the Father also."

When John tells us in Revelation that all liars will have their part in the lake of fire, he is referring to those who lie about Jesus Christ by rejecting Him and His authority as their Lord. The lordship of Christ is brought to bear when John says that such denial is of the antichrist whose very existence is to challenge His lordship. The antichrist is Satan incarnate, and you will recall the challenge that Lucifer made in Isaiah 14:13, having said in his heart, "I will ascend into heaven, I will exalt my throne above the stars of God."

The most infamous liar of all is Lucifer who will be cast into the lake of fire according to Revelation 20:10, "And the devil that deceived them was cast into the lake of fire and brimstone, where the beast and the false prophet are, and shall be tormented day and night forever and ever." Jesus said in John 8:44, "There is no truth in him [Satan]. When he speaketh a lie, he speaketh of his own: for he is a liar, and the father of it."

160

To be clear, those who deny Christ and fail to confess Him as Lord will spend eternity in the lake of fire with the "lord" they have chosen for themselves—Satan. They are the ultimate liars, and their eternal destiny is determined by their own arrogance. Thankfully, no one has to fall into that category. We all have the promise of forgiveness and redemption through the Lord Jesus Christ by confessing Him as our Lord and Savior.

It All Began With Love

When Jesus therefore saw his mother, and the disciple standing by, whom he loved, he saith unto his mother, Woman, Behold thy son! Then saith he to the disciple, Behold thy mother! And from that hour that disciple took her unto his own home.

—John 19:26–27—

The Joy in Knowing Jesus:

As the Father hath loved me, so have I
loved you; continue ye in my love. If ye
keep my commandments, ye shall abide   •
in my love; even as I have kept my Father's
commandments, and abide in his love.
These things have I spoken unto you, that
my joy might remain in you, and that your
joy might be full. [John 15:9–11]

Joy is both a response to love that is given and to love that is received. Jesus promised that "His joy might remain in you" so that "your joy might be full," and that joy is a direct result of His abiding love. In Romans 8:37 we are told that "in all these things we are more than conquerors through him that loved us." Paul goes on to say in verses 38–39, "For I am persuaded, that neither death, nor life, nor angels, nor principalities, nor powers, nor things present, nor things to come, nor height, nor depth, nor any other creature, shall be able to separate us from the love of God, which is in Christ Jesus our Lord."

Without the knowledge of His marvelous love, John reminds us that we would not love God: "We love him, because he first loved us" (1 John 4:19). And without the knowledge of His love, we could not "rejoice with joy unspeakable and full of glory" as 1 Peter 1:8–9 tells us: "[Jesus Christ] Whom having not seen, ye love; in whom, though ye see him not, yet believing, ye have joy unspeakable and full of glory: Receiving the end of your faith, even the salvation of your souls."

165

Our opening heading cited John 15:9–11, but Jesus continued in verses 12–14, "This is my commandment, That ye love one another, as I have loved you. Greater love hath no man than this, that a man lay down his life for his friends. Ye are my friends, if ye do whatsoever I command you." This is the second Great Commandment according to 1 John 3:23, the first being "that we should believe on the name of his [God's] Son Jesus Christ." This is the true meaning of Jesus' words in Matthew 22:37 where He said, "Thou shalt love the Lord thy God with all thy heart, and with all thy soul, and with all thy mind."

The fact is that if you don't believe in the Son of God, our Lord Jesus Christ, then you simply do not "love the Lord your God." Jesus explains it this way: "For the Father himself loveth you, *because ye have loved me, and have believed that I came out from God*" (John 16:27). That is, after all, the first confession that Nicodemus made to our Lord: "Rabbi," he said, "we know that thou art a teacher come from God: for no *man* can do these miracles that thou doest, except God be with him" (John 3:2).

That was the giant step that Nicodemus took to finding *the way* of the cross—the way that is discovered by the new birth. Jesus told Nicodemus, "Verily, verily, I say unto thee, Except a man be born again, he cannot see the kingdom of God" (verse 3).

Then He told Nicodemus that "God so loved the world, that he gave his only begotten Son, that whosoever believeth in him should not perish, but have everlasting *life*" (verse 16). And finally, he told Nicodemus, "But he that doeth *truth* cometh to the light, that his deeds may be made manifest, that they are wrought in God" (verse 21). You see, Nicodemus was the first man in John's Gospel to hear that Christ is indeed "the way, the truth, and the life."

The words of Jesus were enough to inspire that lawyer and ruler of the Jews to dare to defend Christ publicly before the Sanhedrin Council. The Master's words had hit home among the Jews. Some declared, "Of a truth this is the Prophet. Others said, This is the Christ. But some said, Shall Christ come out of Galilee?" (John 19:40–41).

Verses 45–52 give this account: "Then came the officers to the chief priests and Pharisees; and they said unto them, Why have ye not brought him [Jesus]? The officers answered, Never man spake like this man. Then answered them the Pharisees, Are ye also deceived? *Have any of the rulers or of the Pharisees believed on him*? But this people who knoweth not the law are cursed. Nicodemus saith unto them, (he that came to Jesus by night, being one of them,) Doth our law judge any man, before it hear him, and know what he doeth? They answered and said unto him, Art thou also of Galilee?"

Nicodemus was one of those rulers—one of those Pharisees—who evidently believed on Him, for Nicodemus joined Joseph of Arimathæa at the cross to take the body of Jesus. "And there came also Nicodemus, which at the first came to Jesus by night, and brought a mixture of myrrh and aloes, about an hundred pound weight. Then took they the body of Jesus, and wound it in linen clothes with the spices, as the manner of the Jews is to bury" (John 19:39–40). The love of God had worked a miracle in the life of that lawyer.

We have already seen that "we love Him *because* He first loved us." Clearly, then, we cannot love God if we don't love His Son and believe that He came out from God! I will discuss this in greater detail later in this section.

John's writings are rooted in the all-encompassing and everlasting love of God expressed through the life, death, and resurrection of Christ, as well as His promised return for His Church. The two great commandments lay the foundation of John's writings, and John 3:16 is the cornerstone of the New Covenant. Together they set the standard for John's Gospel and his three epistles.

The first reference to love in John's Gospel is, of course, John 3:16: "For God so loved the world, that he gave his only begotten Son, that whosoever believeth in him should nor perish, but have everlasting life." This verse sums up all of the Scriptures that tell us why Jesus came to be crucified and raised from the dead. You will remember when God created the world, the universe, and all living creatures, He saw that it was very good. He loved His creation, and that is the scope of John 3:16. The word *world* is the Greek word *kosmos*, which means *His whole creation*—the universe and everything in it. His desire is to redeem all of it!

In John 6:38–40, Jesus said, "For I came down from heaven, not to do mine own will, but the will of him that sent me. And this is the Father's will which hath sent me, that of all which he hath given me I should lose nothing, but should raise it up again at the last day. And this is the will of him that sent me, that every one which seeth the Son, and believeth on him, may have everlasting life: and I will raise him up at the last day."

Clearly, the will of God is to raise up everyone who puts his faith in Jesus Christ at the last day. The reason for that resurrection is that God loves His children. John tells us in 1 John 3:1–2, "Behold, what *manner of love* the Father hath bestowed upon us, that we should be called the sons [children] of God: therefore the world knoweth us not, because it knew him not. Beloved, now are we the sons of God, and it doth not yet appear what we shall be: but we know that, when he shall appear [*the last day when we shall be raised up to everlasting life*], we shall be like him; for we shall see him as he is." Verse 1 tells us that we can be called the children of God because He loves us so much that He adopts us into His family! We are a small part of His kosmos, yet we are the focal point of His redemption.

People often recite John 3:16 without any thought of the indescribable love and overwhelming compassion God has shown for those who commit their lives to Christ Jesus as Lord. I'll never forget the popular *Laugh In* show several decades ago when Billy Graham was invited to "say whatever he wanted to the television audience." Mr. Graham looked directly into the camera and recited John 3:16. The camera immediately switched to a Nazi-helmeted comedian, Artie Johnson, who grinned and mockingly said, "Ver-r-y interesting." He reflected the same attitude that many deign to express who call themselves Christians today. To many who think they are saved, the verse means no more than a memory verse we are supposed to be able to quote when called upon to do so. Pity the soul that doesn't fully comprehend the love of God!

Let me drive home to you the full meaning of God's love for you as divulged in John 3:16. Suppose you have a child who is as loving, obedient, and well-behaved as a child could possibly be, a child that you love more than life itself, and you see another person who is as vile a creature as could be found on Earth, perhaps a thief, a murderer, or a rapist. Then you discover that person is going to be put to death for his crimes. Would you be willing to trade your child's life for the criminal—especially when you find out that your child would first be tortured unmercifully and literally nailed to a tree until his life is drained from his body? God did! That's how marvelous God's gift was to you and me. That's how unbounding His love is for us!

What about the rest of God's kosmos? After all, the term refers to His whole creation. Well, Jesus told us that "Heaven and earth shall pass away" in Matthew 24:35 and Luke 21:33. But if Heaven and Earth shall pass away, how are they redeemed? Revelation 21:1 explains it: "And I saw a new heaven and a new earth: for the first heaven and the first earth were passed away. And I John saw the holy city, new Jerusalem, coming down from God out of heaven, prepared as a bride adorned for her husband." So you see, God's entire creation will be redeemed, and that redemption is linked directly to His love—for God so loved the *kosmos* that He gave his only begotten Son.

It was the incomparable love of Christ that moved Him to say from the cross, "Father forgive them; for they know not what they do" (Luke 23:34). And it was that same love that brought joy to His heart as the writer of Hebrews explains when he tells us to "run with patience the race that is set before us, Looking unto Jesus, the author and finisher of our faith; who for *the joy* that was set before him endured the cross, despising the shame, and is set down at the right hand of the throne of God" (Hebrews 12:1–2).

It was the unquenchable love of Jesus that brought Him back to Bethany where the Jews were waiting to stone Him to death. It was the lack of belief on the part of Martha who said to Jesus, "Lord, if thou hadst been here, my brother had not died" (John 11:21), and Mary when she "was come where Jesus was, and saw him, she fell down at his feet, saying unto him, Lord, if thou hadst been here, my brother had not died" (v.32), and those who mourned with them that caused Him to "groan in the spirit [Greek: *sigh with indignation*]" when He saw them weeping, and it was that same love that caused Him to weep for them. They all saw in His weeping the love outpoured for Lazarus, not realizing it was their unbelief that brought the tears to His eyes (see John 11:33– 35). But Jesus loved them in spite of their unbelief!

Again, some of the mourners made the accusation, "Could not this man, which opened the eyes of the blind, have caused that even this man should not have died?" (John 11:37). Then "Jesus therefore groaned [*sighed with indignation*] in himself" when He came to the grave.

Then there was the case of the rich young ruler. It was the undying mercy of Christ's love for this young man who knelt before Him thinking that he had kept all of the law. "Then Jesus beholding him loved him" (Mark 10:21).

It was His passionate love that caused Him to grieve for those who came to find atonement for their sins and yet rebelled against the prophets and rejected their Messiah causing Him to cry out, "O Jerusalem, Jerusalem, which killest the prophets, and stonest them that are sent unto thee; how often would I have gathered thy children together, as a hen doth gather her brood under her wings, and ye would not!" (Luke 13:34).

Without exception, everyone who came to Jesus weeping received His loving and merciful care. It was His endless love that moved Him to heal the sick, raise the dead, give sight to the blind, cleanse the leper, give life to paralyzed legs, bring peace to a broken heart, and it was that eternal love that led Him to Calvary's cruel cross, for "greater love hath no man than this, that a man lay down his life for his friends" (John 15:13).

The word *love* appears 114 times in John's writings, and it's no wonder. John sensed a special relationship with the Lord Jesus. Even the disciples were aware of this. After Jesus had washed His disciples' feet, He told them that one of them would betray Him. "Then the disciples looked one on the other, doubting of whom he spake. Now there was leaning on Jesus' bosom one of his disciples, *whom Jesus loved*. Simon Peter therefore beckoned to him, that he should ask who it should be of whom he spake. He then lying on Jesus' breast saith unto him, Lord, who is it? Jesus answered, He it is, to whom I shall give a sop, when I have dipped it" (John 13:22–26).

No one else dared to pose the question to Jesus, especially not Peter, but Peter could ask the disciple whom Jesus loved to do so. John was, after all, that close to Jesus—so close that he was at total liberty to lean on Jesus' bosom at the last supper they were to share together.

Later, as Jesus looked down from the cross, "when He saw his mother, and *the disciple* standing by, *whom*

172

he loved, he saith unto his mother, Woman, behold thy son! Then saith he to the disciple, Behold thy mother! And from that hour that disciple took her unto his own home" (John 19:26–27).

What a marvelous relationship our Lord and young John had with each other! The rest of the disciples failed the Lord completely. They all forsook Him when He was taken by the great multitude who came with swords and staves to take Jesus away (Mark 14:50). They all forsook Him when He was being judged. They all forsook Him when He was crucified—all but John. John was there with Mary at the foot of the cross, no doubt holding Mary close.

You see. John was the disciple whom Jesus loved, and "love never fails," as the Apostle Paul would later tell us in 1 Corinthians 13:8. I can see the eyes of John gazing up into the Savior's eyes and our Lord's eyes gazing into John's as he said, "Behold thy mother." What an honor! What love!

After the resurrection, when Mary Magdalene ran to tell the disciples that the body of Jesus was gone, John tells us that "she runneth, and cometh to Simon Peter, and to *the other disciple, whom Jesus loved*" (John 20:2). These were the two men who seemed to be closer to Jesus than the other disciples, but John was the youngest and perhaps the most in need of guidance and counsel. After all, if John were to look to Peter for such guidance, he would have to look past Peter's lack of consistency where his faith was concerned. Peter was quick to admonish the Lord when Jesus knelt to wash Peter's feet, and he did deny Christ before the crucifixion. His tendency was to speak before thinking. That, of course, is a major problem for most of us!

173

When Mary told them that the body of Jesus was gone from the tomb, Peter and John ran to see for themselves, but John was more anxious to find out what had happened than Peter, and he outran the older disciple to look in the tomb. Peter wasn't anxious to face anything knowing what he had done before the crucifixion. The most impressive thing to see in John was that his love for the Master was unstoppable. John 20:8 tells us that after Peter entered the tomb "then went in also that other disciple [John], which came first to the sepulchre, and he saw, and believed."

What did he believe, and why did he believe it? I have no doubt that He remembered what Jesus had said just before He went to the garden of Gethsemane to pray. In John 14:1, Jesus told His disciples, "Let not your heart be troubled: ye believe in God, believe also in me." John believed. Then Jesus went on to say, "In my Father's house are many mansions [dwelling places]: if it were not so I would have told you. I go to prepare a place for you." John believed Him.

Jesus continued, "And if I go and prepare a place for you, I will come again, and receive you unto myself; that where I am, there ye may be also." I can sense the excitement in John as his heart no doubt pounded, and he believed every word Jesus had spoken. John loved the Master because the Master loved him and always kept John close to Himself. Of all the disciples, the disciple whom Jesus loved would have leaned on every word His Lord said.

Now, one can read the verse in John 20 when John went into the sepulchre, "he saw and believed," that he believed Mary's report that the body was gone. That was obvious because the body really was gone. But there is a reason God wanted us to know that John believed. After all, Peter believed the body was gone, as did Mary Magdalene, but the Bible doesn't add that little comment, "Peter believed," or that "Mary believed." No, there was something special about the fact that John believed. I think the something special was that he believed what Jesus told him: "I go to prepare a place for you. And if I go and prepare a place or you, I will come again, and receive you unto myself; that where I am, there ye may be also." Love told John, "He's alive!" and love told him, "He's coming again!" What joy must have filled his heart to know that everything Jesus had told him was true!

In John 21 our resurrected Lord confronted Peter with the same question three times, "Simon, son of Jonas, lovest thou me?" After telling Peter about his impending death, He said "Follow me. Then Peter turning about, seeth *the disciple whom Jesus loved* following; which also leaned on his breast at supper and said, Lord, which is he that betrayeth thee? Peter seeing him saith to Jesus, Lord, and what shall this man do? Jesus saith unto him, If I will that he tarry till I come, what is that to thee? Follow thou me" (John 21:15–22).

Little did Peter know that the disciple whom Jesus loved would live long enough to pen the last book of the Bible, *the Revelation of Jesus Christ.* The first church that Jesus addressed in that book was the church of Ephesus to whom Jesus warned, "Nevertheless I have somewhat against thee, because thou hast left thy first love. Remember therefore from whence thou art fallen, and repent, and do the first works, or else I will come unto thee quickly, and will remove thy candlestick [church]

175

out of his place, except thou repent" (Revelation 2:4–5).

Then to the church at Laodicea, the church that is swept up in the false doctrine of the last days, a doctrine known today as "seed" or "greed" theology [see Revelation 4:17], He exhorts, "As many as I love, I rebuke and chastise: be zealous therefore, and repent" (4:19).

Joy Fulfilled:

*And now I come to thee [Heavenly Father];
and these things I speak in the world, that they
[the disciples] might have my joy fulfilled in
themselves.* **[John 17:13]**

Why did Jesus view His coming agony of the cross with joy? As previously mentioned, the explanation rests in 1 Peter1:7–9: "That the trial of your faith, being much more precious than gold that perisheth, though it be tried with fire, might be found unto praise and honour and glory at the appearing of Jesus Christ: Whom having not seen, *ye love*, in whom, though now ye see him not, yet believing, *ye rejoice with joy unspeakable and full of glory*: Receiving the end of your faith, even the salvation of your souls."

That's what Jesus said about the angels. "Likewise, I say unto you, there is *joy* in the presence of the angels of God over one sinner that repenteth" (Luke 15:10). Our Lord found joy in knowing that His crucifixion would bring salvation to multiplied millions who would otherwise perish. In like manner, the angels rejoice with our Lord Jesus Christ in seeing the source of His joy fulfilled! If just that one soul were redeemed, Christ would not have died in vain, and His joy would still have been fulfilled.

John's first epistle was the great love letter of the Bible. He wrote, "And these things we write unto you, that your joy may be full" (1 John 1:4). What things was he talking about? If you read them carefully, the first three verses will thrill your soul! "That which was from the beginning, which we have heard, which we have seen with our eyes, which we have looked upon, and our hands have handled, of the Word of life; (For the life was manifested, and we have seen it, and bear witness, and shew unto you that eternal life, which was with the Father, and was manifested unto us;) That which we have seen and heard declare we unto you, that ye also may have fellowship with us: and truly our fellowship is with the Father, and with his Son Jesus Christ."

From the very first time they laid eyes upon the Lord Jesus Christ, from the very beginning of that loving relationship and having actually touched the Living Word, the Word of life, the Lord Jesus Himself, the disciples knew what it meant to have eternal life and to have real fellowship with Jesus Christ, the Son of God, and His Father! Why, they personally witnessed all of the miracles and even shared in them. I'm sure John thought about the time he and Peter had gone to the temple after Jesus had ascended to His Father's house and found the lame man sitting at the gate begging for alms. The two disciples actually applied what the Master had taught them about faith. Peter said, "Look on us. Silver and gold have I none; but such as I have give I thee: In the name of Jesus Christ of Nazareth rise up and walk" (Acts 3:4, 6). Think of it! What they had seen Jesus do, they could now do! The Living Word had told them that after He had ascended to the Father, they would do even greater things than He had done. What joy! What rejoicing! Isn't that what Paul tells us in 1 Thessalonians 2: 19–20? "For what is our hope, or joy, or crown of rejoicing? Are not even ye in the presence of our Lord Jesus Christ at his coming?" It's the same joy that caused him to tell the Philippian believers in Philippians 4:1, "Therefore, my brethren dearly beloved and longed for, my joy and crown, so stand fast in the Lord, my dearly beloved."

Now John is telling us that we, too, can share in the fellowship of the Father and His Son and bear the same witness of eternal life! Think of it! You can lead a person to Jesus Christ and eternal life. There can be no greater reason for joy in your heart—just to know that a man, woman, or child who was destined to perish will spend eternity with our Lord and all those who've confessed Him as their Lord and Savior. That will be your joy and crown of rejoicing.

You might ask, "How is that greater than what Jesus did?" I'm told that the immediate ministry of our Lord was contained within a 70 mile radius, yet the gospel has been spread to every nation on the earth. Television and radio have been valuable tools in spreading the Good News, Billy Graham preached the message of hope and salvation around the world, and missionaries having carried the Word of God to the far corners of this world. A multitude of Christian men and women have given their lives so that others could be saved in every nation. Those are the greater works! But I must confess that none of these "greater works" would ever have been accomplished without the sacrifice of the Lamb of God and the outpouring of His Spirit to every believer.

The Groundswell of Joy:

*But let every man take heed
how he buildeth thereupon. For
other foundation can no man lay
than that is laid, which is Jesus
Christ.* [1Corinthians 3:10–11]

Joy springs from the taproot and cornerstone of faith. A tree cannot live without its taproot; neither can a building stand without its foundation, chief of which is its cornerstone.

The Apostle Paul spoke of his personal joy at seeing the spiritual strength of the Colossian believers. He said, "For though I be absent in the flesh, yet I am with you in the spirit, joying and beholding your order [or *dignity*] and the steadfastness [*unmoveablility*] of your faith in Christ. As ye have therefore received Christ Jesus the Lord, so walk ye in him: *Rooted and built up* in him, and stablished in the faith, as ye have been taught, abounding therein with thanksgiving" (Colossians 2:5–7). No one who calls himself a Christian can deny that Jesus Christ is the foundation, the Chief Cornerstone, of all that we are and can be.

The way of the cross is both orderly and unshakeable. A follower of Christ will move forward in his mission with determination because his roots are established in his faith in Christ, but those roots are grounded in what the whole message of salvation is about. Paul said in Ephesians 3:14–19, "For this cause I bow my knees unto the Father of our Lord Jesus Christ, Of whom the whole family in heaven and earth is named, That he would grant you, according to the riches of his glory, to be strengthened with might by his Spirit in the inner man; That Christ may dwell in your hearts by faith; that ye being *rooted and grounded in love*, May be able to comprehend with all saints what is the breadth, and length, and depth, and height; And to know the love of Christ, which passeth knowledge, that ye might be filled with all the fulness of God."

Our Lord knows how to describe His love. You may remember the old spiritual that says: "His love is so high you can't get over it, so low you can't get under it, so wide you can't get around it. You must go in at the door." It came from the passage above. We are rooted and grounded in love because it's impossible to circumnavigate the love of God. That's the same love that establishes our faith.

What is it that is so important to us that we must have great faith to accomplish it? I can tell you without blinking an eye that if it isn't to express our love for, or obedience to, Christ, then it has nothing to do with faith. Faith is a response to His love. "We love him, because he first loved us" (1 John 4:19). That is the foundation of our faith. Did you ever wonder why the love chapter in Paul's writings, 1 Corinthians 13, ends with, "And now abideth [*remains* or *endures*] faith, hope, love, these three; but the greatest of these is love?" The Authorized Version uses the word "charity" instead of "love," but the correct translation is *love*.

Faith and hope are "joined at the hip." The writer of Hebrews said, "Now faith is the substance of things hoped for, the evidence of things not seen" (Hebrews 11:1). And what is that unseen thing that supplies the evidence? *Love*! Faith and hope are entirely dependent upon love. They are our *present* needs and will no longer be necessary when we enter into eternity. They will be fulfilled at Heaven's gate! But love will march right through the gate and will go on forever.

Faith is never intended to be used to get things that will satisfy our worldly desires. It is intended for us to express our love to our Lord Jesus Christ and to enable us to accomplish His will and His purpose. That's why we are told in 1 John 5:14–15, "And this is the confidence [faith] that we have in him, that, if we ask anything *according to his will*, he heareth us: And if we know that he hear us, whatsoever we ask, we know that we have the petitions that we desired of him."

After describing the worldly struggles we have, struggles that hinder our prayers, James said, "Ye ask, and receive not, because ye ask amiss, that ye may consume it upon your lusts [or you ask for it just to use it for your own worldly pleasures]" (James 4:3).

When my wife, Jeanette, and I bought our house there was a Bradford pear tree stump in the backyard that wouldn't die. Its roots had spread throughout the yard causing its shoots to spring up like weeds—dozens and dozens of tiny trees that would rebound after every mowing. I spent months chopping at the stump with an axe and poured salt into its wounds. Friends and neighbors made many suggestions, tricks they had learned through the years that were surefire ways to kill the tree—all to no avail. We were cursed with an unwanted stump with its myriads of little fledglings thriving in our lawn. When it rained the numbers grew to double and triple the tiny saplings.

Finally, in desperation, I dug around the stump, going deeper and deeper to locate the taproot. After a lot of digging and pounding, I hit solid wood and began chopping more fervently. The wood was about eight inches in diameter, and it seemed that it took forever to hack my way through it. Finally, the axe hit dirt beneath the wood. The root didn't grow downward as I had thought a taproot would, but it spread straight out from the stump. The little trees continued to grow. It took a Bobcat blade and a concrete driveway to put an end to my little forest!

The next year, a windstorm split the remaining tree in my front yard, and I had it cut down. Alas! I had another stump to deal with and another growth of little trees! Fortunately, I met a man who operated a "tree stump removal service," and for fifty dollars it took twenty minutes for the stump to become sawdust.

Sometimes faith and wisdom are inseparable. I suppose it was a kind of faith that told me, in spite of two heart attacks and six stents in my arteries (now seven), that I could remove the stump in the backyard, taproot, and miniature forest myself, but had wisdom prevailed, I would have called a tree stump removal serviceman, tossed in fifty dollars, and solved my problem in twenty minutes. My joy and rejoicing would have come much quicker, and I would have saved months of stress on my heart and quandaries about my faith!

An unusual conversation took place between Christ and His apostles in Luke 17:3–10. It began with instructions from the Lord concerning forgiveness. "Take heed to yourselves. If thy brother trespass against thee, rebuke him; and if he repent, forgive him. And if he trespass against thee seven times in a day, and seven times in a day turn again to thee, saying, I repent; thou shalt forgive him" (3,4).

What would you do if someone did harm to you or your reputation, then later came to you and said, "I'm sorry, please forgive me"? You might be slow to do so, but probably you would say, "Oh, forget it. We all make mistakes" But what would you do if this happened seven times in one day? I would be prone to think, "This man has some serious problems, and if I want to keep a good reputation, I'd better keep my distance."

But the Lord said, "If he repents, forgive him." That must have seemed like a heavy load to bear to the apostles because they "said unto the Lord, Increase our faith" (5).

Jesus responded, "If ye had faith as a grain of mustard seed, ye *might* say unto this sycamine tree, Be thou plucked up by the root, and be thou planted in the sea; and it *should* obey you" (Luke 17:5–6). Now any intelligent person would realize that Jesus wasn't endorsing the idea that we should go around demanding that trees be plucked up and transplanted to the sea, anymore than He expected us to use our faith to cause mountains to fly through the air and splash down in the sea in Matthew 21:21 or dropped on southern plantations [yonder places] as we read in Matthew 17:20.

No, Jesus was rebuking them for their unwillingness to obey His instructions. He placed the onus on the disciples: "If *you* had faith—If *you* had the tiniest bit of faith, like a grain of mustard seed, *you* might say to this sycamine tree. . . ." Now most people stop reading at this point. I suppose they might consider my own experience with the stump and assume that I could have simply said to the stump in my yard, "Remove thyself into my neighbor's yard," and poof! It would have leaped into the air and burrowed into the yard next door causing much grief to my neighbor. If that was what faith really meant, Christians would cause absolute chaos in the world just to get everything they demanded!

That isn't what the Lord was saying at all, and it's why we must always read the context of every verse of Scripture. Jesus used the illustration of the master and his servant to explain their problem—not a lack of faith, but a lack of judgment, compassion, and wisdom.

He said, "But which of you, having a servant plowing or feeding cattle, will say unto him by and by, when he is come from the field, Go and sit down to meat? And will not rather say unto him, Make ready wherewith I may sup, and gird thyself, and serve me, till I have eaten and drunken; and afterward thou shalt eat and drink? Doth he thank that servant because he did the things that were commanded him? I trow not [Greek: *I think not*]. So likewise ye, when ye shall have done all those things which are commanded you, say, We are unprofitable servants: we have done that which was our duty to do" (Luke 17:7–10).

Rather than ask for more faith, the apostles should have put into action what the Lord had taught them all along. If "His mercy endures forever," as the Psalmist declared on numerous occasions, then it is the responsibility of every believer to elicit that same mercy. How many times have you found yourself asking God to forgive you for something you've done before many times—each time, repenting, confessing, and asking for forgiveness? I know I have! But if we can be forgiven so many times, why shouldn't we fulfill our responsibility to do the same? It doesn't take increased faith to forgive; it takes love—the foundation of our faith—and compassion.

You see, instead of the apostles asking the Lord to increase their faith, they should have been *applying* their faith. Faith is a duty, not an award. Certainly you can't increase a person's faith by turning the thermostat up, nor can you slap him in the head and pronounce that his faith is now increased! Faith is what you put into action—spurred on by the love of God, not a mortal feeling or talent.

There is no reference anywhere in the New Testament that says God will increase our faith. Faith is faith. You either have it, or you don't. Don't you think it's strange that people can have the faith to believe they are going to Heaven but not that God will assist them in their accomplishments for the cause of Christ, His glory, and His kingdom in this life?

We often confuse the *application* of our faith with the *volume* of that faith, as though the Lord parcels out faith by increments. Did God give me a bucket-full of faith, a bushel, or a freight car full of faith, or did He give me faith and leave it up to me as to whether or not I will use it? In Matthew 8:5–13, when Jesus was approached by a Roman centurion, a commander of a hundred soldiers, and told Jesus that his servant was sick with the palsy and "grievously tormented" (verse 5), the Lord offered to come and heal the servant.

The centurion, being a Gentile, said, "Lord, I am not worthy that thou shouldst come under my roof: but speak the word only, and my servant shall be healed" (verse

8). After all, said he, "I am a man under authority, having soldiers under me: and I say to this man, Go, and he goeth; and to another, Come, and he cometh; and to my servant, Do this, and he doeth it." In other words, the centurion explained that he understood the difference between ordering someone else to do something, but never could he order someone who was by far his superior. As a Roman soldier, he could not stoop to requiring the Jewish Messiah to do his bidding. Instead, he applied the faith that only Christ's servants could possess by saying, "Speak the word only, and my servant shall be healed" (verse 8).

The Lord's response was, "Verily I say unto you, I have not found so great faith, no, not in Israel" (verse 10). Jesus came unto His own, but His own failed to receive or believe in Him. This non-Jew expressed the faith that Christ's own people could not, or would not, do. The centurion trusted Christ, believing that He could heal his servant without placing Himself on the Gentile's level. The man had the faith and applied it as every believer should.

It's similar to our relationship with the Holy Spirit. When we repent from sin and confess Christ as our Lord, we are immediately baptized with the Holy Spirit. The Spirit of God then indwells us in all His fulness, yet Paul tells us in Ephesians 5:17–18, "Wherefore be ye not unwise, but understanding what the will of the Lord is. And be not drunk with wine, wherein is excess [the literal Greek translation is: *Be not drunk with wine because that's what the unsaved do*], but be filled with the Spirit."

Paul is comparing our spiritual life with that of an unbeliever! Unbelievers will allow themselves to be controlled by their consumption of alcohol, but Christians must allow themselves to be controlled by the greatest source of power in all the universe—the Holy Spirit. That's the wise thing to do! Not only so, it is *God's will* that we do so. We are possessed by Him in all His fulness, but we tend to apply only what we think we can get by with. By being filled with the Spirit we are making use of, or applying, His fulness in us. That's why John reminds us that "greater is he that is in you, than he that is in the world" (1 John 4:4).

So it is with faith. We use only what we think we can get by with, and if we think we are not good enough to invite Jesus under our roof, just remember Who it is that lives within us already! You see, it is not how much faith we possess but how much we are willing to apply what God has already given us.

Where "faith and the sycamine tree" are concerned, if you really have faith you would believe that you could uproot that sycamine tree by some means apart from wishing it to be uprooted. You could dig it up and cut the taproot, or you could chop the tree down and call a stump removal serviceman to turn the stump into sawdust in just twenty minutes! I suppose you could even set fire to the tree and have the faith to believe you won't set your neighbor's house on fire in the process.

The fact is that faith is not an ethereal entity that indwells a believer. It is the "*substance* of things hope for, the *evidence* of things not seen (Hebrews 11:1). The Greek word translated *substance* literally means "that which stands under [*the foundation*]." It is the foundation for whatever it is that we hope to achieve. In any case, it requires action on your part. Faith tells us that if

188

we think we can't accomplish what needs to be done, do it anyway. Otherwise, you have no faith at all! You see, that's when the Lord steps in to help.

When circumstances are clearly beyond the scope of human strength or ability, our faith is still in God. Psalm 46:1–3 assures us that "God is our refuge and strength, a very present help in trouble. Therefore will not we fear, though the earth be removed, and though the mountains be carried into the midst of the sea; Though the waters thereof roar and be troubled, though the mountains shake with the swelling thereof."

Remember, Paul said that our faith is "rooted and grounded in love," and John tells us that "there is no fear in love; but perfect love casteth out fear: because fear hath torment. He that feareth is not made perfect in love" (1 John 4:18). Colossians 2:6–7 gives this exhortation: "As ye have therefore received Christ Jesus the Lord, so walk ye in him: Rooted and built up in him, and sta-blished in the faith, as ye have been taught, abounding therein with thanksgiving."

The Two Great Commandments, The Law of Christ:

And this is his commandment, that we should believe on the name of his Son Jesus Christ, and love one another, as he gave us commandment. [1 John 3:23]

John's first epistle is based entirely on the two great commandments with, as we have seen, a different application of the first of those commandments. In Matthew 22:34–40, the Pharisees tried to deceive Jesus by having one of their lawyers ask Him a question about the law under Moses. The man asked Him, "Master, which is the great commandment in the law? Jesus said unto him, Thou shalt love the Lord thy God with all thy heart, and with all thy soul, and with all thy mind. This is the first and great commandment. And the second is like unto it, Thou shalt love thy neighbor as thyself. On these two commandments hang all the law and the prophets" (36–40).

Had Jesus said, "Believe in me, the Son of God," He would have been accused of denying the Jewish law, and more. Although His reply would have been the absolute truth, He would have been accused of blasphemy, as He ultimately was. And if he had said, "The second is like unto it, Thou shalt love one another," again, He would have had the same accusation thrown at Him.

In John 13:34, Jesus told His disciples, "A new commandment I give unto you, That ye love one another; as I have loved you, that ye also love one another. By this shall all men know that ye are my disciples, if ye have love one to another." This is the second great commandment, but instead of referring to the Jewish brethren, He directed the commandment to His own followers.

When John said, "And this is his commandment, That we should believe on the name of his Son Jesus Christ," in 1 John 3:23, He was merely stating what "loving the Lord thy God with all thy heart, and with all thy soul, and with all thy mind" really entails—our devotion to the Son of God as our Redeemer and our Lord. If you don't love the Lord Jesus Christ, you don't love God.

The second commandment specifies God's family of believers: "and love one another, as he gave us commandment," remembering that the word "neighbor" is correctly translated "near one." No one can be closer than the children of light, the servants of Christ. Hence, John tells us that we are debtors to each other because we are debtors to Christ. In 1 John 3:16 John reminds us that Christ loved us so much that He gave His life for us, but he said more: "Hereby perceive we the love of God, because he laid down his life for us: and we ought to lay down our lives for the brethren."

Throughout history Christians have died both for Christ and for each other. My wife, who was with her missionary parents in the Belgian Congo, told me about African believers who would surround missionaries to provide protection when Congolese soldiers came though the area pillaging and killing. One needs only to read *Fox's Book of Martyrs* to know what it means to be a real Christian. Those believers expressed the true meaning of the word *love*!

191

1 John 4:7 tells us, "Beloved, let us love one another: for love is of God; and every one that loveth is born of God, and knoweth God." John goes on to remind us that "he that loveth not knoweth not God; for God is love. In this was manifested the love of God toward us, because that God sent his only begotten Son into the world, that we might live through him. Herein is love, not that we loved God, but that he loved us, and sent his Son to be the propitiation [*atonement* brought about by Christ's suffering and death] for our sins. Beloved, if God so loved us, we ought also to love one another" (verses 8–11). If we don't have this kind of love, we are not born of God!

Let's take it a step further. In 1 John 3:17 we are given this admonishment: "But whoso hath this world's good, and seeth his brother have need, and shutteth up his bowels of compassion from him, how dwelleth the love of God in him?"

Here's the issue: As we have already seen, there are two commandments, and only two, for the Christian to keep. Those are spelled out in 1 John 3:23: "And this is his commandment, That we should believe on the name of his Son Jesus Christ, and love one another, as he gave us commandment."

We know that unless you believe on the name of God's only begotten Son, you will spend eternity in the lake of fire! John said, "He that believeth on the Son of God hath the witness [*the Holy Spirit*] in himself: he that believeth not God hath made him a liar; because he believeth not the record that God gave of his Son. And this is the record, that God hath given to us eternal life, and this life is in his Son. He that hath the Son hath life, and he that hath not the Son of God hath not life" (1 John 5:10–12). Who would dare call Almighty God a liar? That's what you do when you don't believe in His Son, the Lord Jesus Christ.

Jesus said, "He that hath my commandments [the same two great commandments], and keepeth them, he it is that loveth me: and he that loveth me shall be loved of my Father, and I will love him, and will manifest myself [*make myself known*] to him" (John 14:21). In verses 23 and 24, Jesus said, "If a man love me, he will keep my words [referring to the two commandments]: and my Father will love him, and we will come unto him, and make our abode with him [again referring to the Holy Spirit]. He that loveth me not keepeth not my sayings."

We see from the above Scriptures that keeping the Great Commandments gives us the privilege of being filled with the Holy Spirit, of experiencing the love of the Father and of the Son, and of Christ manifesting Himself—that is, making Himself known to us.

There are those who believe that the promise Jesus made to His disciples in John 14 regarding answered prayer applies to all believers. But if that is true, then that benefit rests in keeping the two commandments according to John 14:13–15: "And whatsoever ye shall ask in my name, that will I do, that the Father may be glorified in the Son. If ye shall ask any thing in my name, I will do it. If ye love me, keep my commandments." Every time the promise of answered prayer is made by our Lord it is accompanied by the admonition to keep those commandments.

If you wonder why your prayers don't seem to be answered, consider that admonition. Do you truly love the Lord your God with all your heart, with all your soul,

193

with all your mind, and with all your strength, and do you love your Christian brothers and sisters [*your near ones*] as yourself as we are commanded in Matthew 22:37–39, Mark 12:29–31, and 1 John 3:23? If we ask God, "Lord, will you . . . ," then we must listen to His still, small voice, "Do you love me? Do you love mine?"

You see, the way of the cross is the way of love—a love that requires complete devotion to Christ and His Kingdom.

The Way of the Cross
Made Plain:

And you, being dead in your sins
and the uncircumcision of your
flesh, hath he quickened together
with him, having forgiven you all
your trespasses; Blotting out the
handwriting of ordinances that was
against us, which was contrary to us,
and took it out of the way, nailing
it to his cross. **[Colossians 2:13–14]**

Why is the cross so vital to anyone who is not a follower of Christ? Surely, the way of the cross means nothing to those who don't know Christ. And you can't know Christ unless you know who He is or why He allowed Himself to be nailed to that tree.

What does the cross mean to you? Do you wear it from your neck or pin it to your clothes— decked in silver, gold, or gemstones? Is it simply an ornament? Or do you see it as a crown at the top of a church steeple or an emblem on your car bumper? On the other hand, are you offended by the mere appearance of the cross in any setting?

If the cross of Christ means nothing to the unbeliever, then why is it such an offensive symbol? That's like the lunacy of those who say they don't believe in God, yet they spend their lives fighting against God! If you think the cross isn't offensive to the anti-Christian element of this world, you haven't paid attention to the legal hassle the atheists are making of it. A recent debate put on by those enemies of the cross of Christ before the Supreme Court was over the cross-shaped beam that was rescued from the World Trade Center rubble of September 11, 2001. They argued that the presence of that piece of cross-shaped metal literally "makes them sick." How is that possible if it is indeed a meaningless object in their view? If these sons of Satan don't believe in it, why does it upset them so much? Fortunately the decision went in favor of the cross.

The Apostle Paul wrote in 1 Corinthians 1:18, "For the preaching of the cross is to them that perish foolishness; but unto us which are saved it is *the power of God*." Therein lies the answer: if those who hold the cross in contempt are told that rejecting the preaching of the cross will result in their eternal damnation, then, of course, that preaching must be foolishness. To them it is even more foolish if you throw in the fact that Christ rose from the dead and will return to judge the world of the ungodly. They want to remain among the ungodly because they are in rebellion against Almighty God and everything that represents Him in this world. They want to be their own gods—continuing in the footsteps of their predecessors, Adam and Eve, and their father, the devil. They *must* deny the truth of the cross and destroy its presence from society or lose their self-proclaimed power.

Today's opponents of the cross are the same as those to whom Jesus said, "Ye are of your father the devil, and the lusts of your father ye will do. He was a murderer from the beginning, and abode not in the truth, because there is no truth in him. When he speaketh a lie, he speaketh of his own: for he is a liar, and the father of it. And because I tell you the truth, ye believe me not" (John 8:44–45).

Such people don't want to hear the truth. Notice that Jesus said, "Because I tell you the truth, ye believe me not." They don't believe Christ is lying to them. They believe He is telling them the truth, and because they don't want to know the truth, they reject His gospel. They reject the preaching of the cross, and, hence, they reject the "power of God."

That brings us to the second issue in their war of rebellion: "to us which are saved [the cross of Christ] is *the power of God*." That's why those who seem destined for destruction find it so offensive! That's why Paul calls it "the offense of the cross" in Galatians 5:11. By preaching the cross we have the power of the Holy Spirit to change lives and eternal destinies. Paul goes on to say in Galatians 6:14, "But God forbid that I should glory, save in the cross of our Lord Jesus Christ, by whom the world is crucified unto me, and I unto the world."

The power of God is the power of the resurrection. Jesus was slain on the cross, and Paul claimed that death as his own "that I may know him," he said, "and the power of his resurrection, and the fellowship of his sufferings, being made comformable unto his death; If by any means I might attain unto the resurrection of the dead" (Philippians 3:10–11). That's why the cross of Christ is the power of God to those of us who are saved!

The cross represents the sacrifice that the Lord Jesus Christ made on Mount Calvary. There is nothing pretty or flashy about it. It represents the blood He shed for you and me—the blood that cleanses us from all sin and provides atonement for those sins. And it represents the power of God in establishing the Lordship of Jesus Christ God's Son.

The way of the cross begins with the exhortation the Lord gives us in Hebrews 12:1–2, "Wherefore seeing we also are compassed about with so great a cloud of witnesses, let us lay aside every weight, and the sin which doth so easily beset us, and let us run with patience the race that is set before us, Looking unto Jesus the author and finisher of our faith, who for the joy that was set before him endured the cross, despising the shame, and is set down at the right hand of the throne of God."

God gives us a brief history of men and women of faith who gave their lives in His service in chapter 11 as examples for us to follow. That's why He begins chapter 12 with "wherefore." Wherefore, we should follow their examples.

Our first step is to forsake our old nature, the sin that undermines our service for Christ, as well as those things in this world that would override that service. "Let us lay aside every weight [those things in life that consume our time and attention], and the sin which doth so easily beset us." Wicked behavior defeats our purpose. One who is known for his sinful life cannot be a servant for Christ. That's why we often hear the argument, "The church is full of hypocrites. I'm just as good as they are!"

A woman came to my door one afternoon with tears running down her cheeks. "I don't know what to do," she said, "My husband gave me his paycheck and told me to deposit it in the bank, but I lost it."

"Call your husband and have him put a stop payment on it. His employer can do that," was my wise response.

"Oh, no!" she said. "I can't do that! I lost it at the casino!"

That's why so many who call themselves Christians are absolute failures when it comes to their service for Christ. Jesus said, "No servant can serve two masters: for either he will hate the one, and love the other; or else he will hold to the one, and despise the other. Ye cannot serve God and mammon" (Luke 16:13). Your mammon might be money, or worldly activities, or addictions to alcohol, drugs, or sex. They all block the path to the way of the cross!

John said, "Love not the world, neither the things that are in the world. If any man love the world, the love of the Father is not in him" (1 John 2:15). What or who do you love?

You see, the world always blinds the eyes of the double-minded man. James said, "A double minded man is unstable in all his ways" (James 1:8). But he gives the cure for this sickness in 4:8, ""Draw nigh to God, and he will draw nigh to you. Cleanse your hands, ye sinners; and purify your hearts, ye double-minded." He adds in verse 10, "Humble yourselves in the sight of the Lord, and he shall lift you up."

Then the writer of Hebrews tells us to keep our eyes on the One who wrote the book and completes our mission of faith. "Looking unto Jesus the author and finisher of our faith." When we are truly living in the way of the cross, Christ the Lord must always be the Light that guides our pathway and the image for which we strive to follow.

Christ is, after all, the Lord of all of His creation. He is the King of kings and Lord of lords. Unless you recognize this most basic truth, you can never inherit eternal life. His sacrifice on the cross would be meaningless because He would not have the authority to give you that life. It is true that our sins are covered by the blood Jesus shed on the cross, but believe it or not, that isn't the most important reason for His crucifixion! The Lord Jesus Christ went to that cross in order to establish His Lordship over His creation!

Let me remind you that "none of us liveth to himself, and no man dieth to himself. For whether we live, we live unto the Lord; and whether we die, we die unto the Lord: whether we live therefore, or die, we are the Lord's. For to this end Christ both died, and rose, and revived, *that he might be Lord* both of the dead and living" (Romans 14:7–9). Without Christ in your life and in your heart, you are dead—dead in your sins. Until you realize that truth and recognize that Christ is your Lord, you will never receive eternal life.

What about the believer? Why is the cross so vital to every follower of Jesus Christ? What is it about the cross that *requires* our taking it up as our own? The Apostle Paul said, "For Christ sent me not to baptize, but to preach the gospel: not with wisdom of words, lest the cross of Christ should be made of none effect" (1 Corinthians 1:17).When we place our trust in Christ as our Lord and Savior, the path is laid out before each one of us—the way of the cross. That cross is something that we must carry throughout our earthly sojourn, and it isn't an easy road to follow.

"But," you may ask, "what about the promise Jesus made to us in Matthew 11:28–30?" Well, let's examine those verses. Jesus said, "Come unto me, all ye that labour and are heavy laden, and I will give you rest. Take my yoke upon you, and learn of me; for I am meek and lowly in heart: and ye shall find rest unto your souls. For my yoke is easy, and my burden is light."

Those who labor and are heavy laden are weighed down with the burden of sin. The word for *labor* in the Greek literally means *fatigued* or *weary*. *Heavy laden* literally refers to *being weighed down as a beast of burden*. That's a very heavy load to carry.

Jesus tells us to take His yoke upon us. A *yoke* is something that *joins two things together*, but in this case it refers to *a servant being joined with a master*. In other words, they work side by side. There is still work to be done, and there is still a burden to carry. The yoke that binds us together with Christ is the cross. That's why our Lord said in Luke 9:23, "If any man will come after me, let him deny himself, and take up his cross daily, and follow [Greek: *be in the same way* or *accompany*] me." The difference between the lost sinner and the follower of Christ is that the sinner plods along by himself bearing an extemely heavy load, while the Christian walks along with Jesus, and they share the load together.

Most people misinterpret these verses based on today's evangelical church's attempt to make salvation and the Christian life too simple—too easy. That's why people so often think that if they just "went forward" during the invitation time, it's enough "work" to get them a free pass to Heaven. Or perhaps they think because they repeat a prayer after the preacher they get their passport to Heaven stamped. They might say, "That's enough work for today." Of course, there's always baptism or communion to put a final seal of approval on one's salvation. Surely, if one has accomplished all of these acts (works), they've guaranteed their spot in Heaven! Then again, there are those who nod their heads when the preacher tells them all they need to do is "accept Jesus as their Savior," and their work is all finished. They can go on their merry way, behaving the same way they did before they made that naive profession!

In such a case, they would be no different from a man named Demas who traveled with the Apostle Paul. Demas was evidently one who thought works could save him. But the truth will out! In 2 Timothy 4:10, Paul said, "Demas hath forsaken me, having loved this present world, and is departed."

Let me state emphatically that none of those conditions for salvation are found anywhere in the Bible— God's Holy Word! And if it isn't in the Bible, it is simply not true. There are no acts of man's making that will save a soul. Salvation rests in one's relationship with Jesus Christ! It's a matter of commitment to Him and not the world.

Ephesians 2:8–9 gives these words of wisdom, "For by grace are ye saved through faith; and that not of yourselves: it is the gift of God: Not of works, lest any man should boast." Think about it. If you can be saved by going forward, or repeating someone else's prayer, or "accepting Christ," or even by being baptized, that all constitutes "works!" It all depends on your own behavior. God has no say in the matter! But Ephesians 2:9 flatly states that salvation is not by works.

On the other hand, verse 10 tells us that we are "[God's] workmanship, created [by God] in Christ Jesus unto good works, which God hath before ordained that we should walk in them." Those are works that are established by the Lord and not by you. According to verse 8, the works are "not of yourselves." They are God's work of salvation as a gift. "For by grace [God's grace] are ye saved through faith [your faith].

In fact, if we back up to verses 4–7, we'll see how precisely God puts it. "But God, who is rich in mercy, for his great love wherewith he loved us, Even when we were *dead* in sins, hath quickened us [*given us life*] together with Christ, (by grace ye are saved;) And has raised us up together, and made us sit together in heavenly places in Christ Jesus: That in the ages to come he might shew the exceeding riches of his grace in his kindness toward us through Christ Jesus."

Paul says that we are dead in sins without Christ. A dead man cannot decide to sit up in his coffin and declare himself to be alive. Only God can give life to a dead man. It took Christ to call out "Lazarus come forth" before a man who had been dead for days to walk out of his tomb alive and well (John 11:43). Lazarus could never have raised himself! It took Jesus to say "Talitha Cumi [damsel, arise], before the young daughter of the ruler of the synagogue could come to life from the dead (Mark 5:41).

Jesus made it clear when He said, "No man can come to me, except the Father which hath sent me draw him: and I will raise him up at the last day" (John 6:44). You can't be saved by finding Christ acceptable to you. He must find you acceptable to Him, and that is accomplished by your yielding to the calling of God to give your life to Christ. That's where your faith comes in. You must trust God to do what He said He would do. While salvation is offered by grace alone, you have to "believe in your heart that God has raised His Son from the dead"

203

and be willing to be bought with the price of blood—the blood that Jesus shed on the cross. "For ye are bought with a price: therefore glorify God in your body, and in your spirit, which are God's" (1 Corinthians 6:20). That makes Christ the Lord of your life. You have become His purchased possession.

Notice that everything about your salvation is accomplished by God through Christ—not by you! That's why Paul tells us "That if thou shalt confess with thy mouth Jesus as Lord, and shalt believe in thine heart that God hath raised him from the dead, thou shalt be saved" (Romans 10:9). You see, there is no work involved at all in making such a confession. Speaking the words doesn't cause you to put forth any effort! And there is certainly no work involved in believing that God has raised Christ from the dead. It only requires you to have confidence that what God said is true! God has the sole responsibility of saving you by His marvelous grace. Rather than your accepting Him as your Savior, *God* "hath made *us* accepted in the beloved" (Ephesians 1:6). He must be your Lord in order for Him to be your Savior.

So you see, those who tell you that so-called "Lordship salvation" is salvation by works are lying to you. They know that their own position of salvation by "accepting Jesus" is actually salvation by works. Such a view places you as being solely responsible for your salvation. That's works—not grace!

Now you may ask, "Why the cross?" The cross has been inappropriately carried by armies throughout history to put down the heathen hordes of other countries. And as I mentioned at the beginning, it has been used as an ornament hanging from ladies' necks, lapel pins, table decorations, book emblems, and monuments. But none of these represent the truth embodied in the cross of Christ. The cross that the Romans used to rid the Roman empire of unwanted people—whether they were criminals, political enemies, or followers of Christ—was a horrible way of killing off unwanted citizens.

The cross of Christ, however, was much more than that. The sins of every man, woman, and child were nailed to the cross through the hands and feet of the Son of God. Everyone born into this world carries the stigma of sin and death. That's a curse that resulted from Adam and Eve's rebellion in the Garden of Eden. David declared in Psalm 51:5 that he was conceived in his mother's womb as a sinner. And that is true of everyone. Paul said in Romans 5:12, "Wherefore, as by one man [Adam] sin entered into the world, and death by sin; and so death passed upon all men, for that all have sinned." Is it any wonder, then, that death was to be overcome by the death of God's Son on the cross? Christ took that curse and placed it upon Himself! Then everlasting life became a reality with the resurrection of Christ from the dead.

Life! A new life begins the moment you confess Christ as your Lord and receive Him as your Savior. The sting of death is erased. How is that possible? After all, our body will still die. The difference is that we are passed from death to life by the blood that was spilled on the cross. "[God] hath saved us, and called us with an holy calling, not according to our works, but according to his own purpose and grace, which was given us in Christ Jesus before the world began, But is now made manifest by the appearing of our Saviour Jesus Christ, who hath *abolished death*, and hath *brought life and immortality to light* through the gospel" (2 Timothy 1:9–10). In other words, this body will still die, but we will have eternal life in the kingdom of God because of the sacrifice Christ made for us. He took our sins and claimed them as His own.

By confessing Christ as our Lord and Savior, we can declare with Paul, "Likewise reckon ye also yourselves to be dead indeed unto sin, but alive unto God through Jesus Christ our Lord" (Romans 6:11). On the other hand, those who reject Christ will spend eternity in the lake of fire with the devil and his angels. That's a decision that every living soul must make for himself. "For the wages of sin is death; but the gift of God is eternal life through Jesus Christ our Lord" (Romans 6:23).

We read in Galatians 3:13, "Christ hath redeemed us from the curse of the law, being made a curse for us: for it is written, Cursed is every one that hangeth on a tree." The cross was the tree on which our Lord bore our curse.

The cross of Christ has been condemned, defamed, and made a subject of ridicule. It has in these wicked days been removed from public places, cursed, and made an object of man's scorn. Let me repeat Paul's reminder that "the preaching of the cross is to them that perish foolishness; but unto us which are saved it is the power of God" (1 Corinthians 1:18).

Once again, Hebrews 12:2 admonishes us that we should be "Looking unto Jesus the author and finisher of our faith; who for the joy that was set before him endured the cross, despising the shame, and is set down at the right hand of the throne of God."

Why the cross? Because Jesus has made peace with us through the blood of His cross according to Colossians 1:20. Christ took your weight of sins upon Himself, nailed them to the cross, and said "*It is finished*!" (John 19:30).

19783641R00132

Made in the USA
Middletown, DE
04 May 2015